ENDORSEMENTS

"Some books make you feel like you are right there with the author. *Going After More: Leaving Limitations to Pursue the God of Possibilities* is one of those books. Kiersten's descriptive writing paints a vivid picture. Using her experiences, including the whispers of God, she takes you to places you couldn't get to on your own and lights a path for you to join God for more. It's amazing how one person's path can help you make sense of your own. This book has helped me piece some of the confusing parts of my life into a clearer picture. If you want to stay stuck, skip the book but don't forget you were invited. If you want to be inspired, *Going After More* is a must-read."

SHELL COWPER-SMITH Parent/Family/Youth Coach

"I have had the pleasure of knowing Kiersten since we were children, and she has always been a person of integrity, passion, and joy. In her first book, *Going After More: Leaving Limitations to Pursue the God of Possibilities,* Kiersten unpacks kingdom revelations that bring breakthrough, strength, and hope to the reader. Her writing style is clear, her stories are incredibly relatable and there were countless phrases throughout the book worthy of underlining and re-reading, as the thought being communicated was Spirit and Life, not just words on a page. I believe this book is a key to impart courage to relinquish the lesser for the glories of the greater that God has for every son and daughter."

BETHANY HICKS, author of *Own Your Assignment* and *The God Connection, Co-founder of Prophetic Company*

"Kiersten brings her whole heart to this book. She gives the reader an authentic look into the journey of someone who could not settle for "going through life in a mediocre way," a statement that resonates with something in all of us. Woven throughout these pages, you will find threads of hope and encouragement but at the core of Kiersten's story is her testimony of the goodness of God, frequently found in both the mundane and the sublime. There are so many great nuggets to take away from this book. What spoke to me most is that there is no such thing as an ordinary life when it has been given to God. I pray as you read this book, your heart will be ignited afresh to pursue the One who loves you the most."

RACHEL CARROLL, author of *The Voice of Love: Learning the Heart of Prophecy*, Co-Founder of Building Contenders

"Going After More captures your heart from the very first pages. Kiersten Clegg has a way of inviting the reader immediately into her story, where you find your *own* story written in between the lines. Through the twists and turns of life, the unexpected, and the disappointments, we find that resounding question *Is there more?* Kiersten masterfully takes us through her journey of answering that question throughout life's experiences and leaves us with a profound answer - that indeed, there is. She vulnerably shares powerful truths that anyone can engage with as if you were sitting across from her with a cup of coffee in hand. You will feel stirred in your own heart with each chapter to go after more!

HEATHER NUNN, Worship Leader, Speaker, Author

Have you settled for less than God's best for your life? Have you stopped short of obtaining all that God has for you? In reading "Going After More" we are challenged to look deep within and discover areas where we have settled because we were not seeing the fruit in our lives that we wanted to see. We are reminded that delay is not denial, or as Kiersten points out in this timely book, it is in those moments of delay that "patience opens a door into the more that is waiting for us. Patience propels us forward". As pastors to Kiersten, we have known her prophetic voice to our church and now with this book, we believe her prophetic voice will bring timely wisdom to you. You will be encouraged not to settle for "just enough" but through a better understanding of patience, perspective, intimacy with God, and hunger you will find out how to go after "more than enough." This book is a must-read if you feel like there has to be more to life than what you are experiencing right now, or if you want to add fuel to the fire already burning.

BEN AND KATIE BRINKMAN, Lead Pastors, Canvas Church

GOING AFTER

More

LEAVING LIMITATIONS TO PURSUE
THE GOD OF POSSIBILITIES

KIERSTEN CLEGG

Scripture quotations marked (AMP) are taken from the Amplified Bible, Copyright © 1954, 1958, 1962, 1964, 1965, 1987 by The Lockman Foundation. Used with permission.

Scripture quotations marked (CEV) are from the Contemporary English Version Copyright © 1991, 1992, 1995 by American Bible Society. Used by Permission.

Scripture quotations marked (MSG) are taken from The Message, copyright © 1993, 2002, 2018 by Eugene H. Peterson. Used by permission of NavPress. All rights reserved. Represented by Tyndale House Publishers.

Scripture quotations marked (NIV) are taken from the Holy Bible, New International Version®, NIV®. Copyright © 1973, 1978, 1984, 2011 by Biblica, Inc.® Used by permission of Zondervan. All rights reserved worldwide. www.zondervan.com The "NIV" and "New International Version" are trademarks registered in the United States Patent and Trademark Office by Biblica, Inc.®

Scripture quoted by permission. Quotations designated (NET) are from the NET Bible® copyright ©1996, 2019 by Biblical Studies Press, L.L.C. http://netbible.com. All rights reserved.

Scripture quotations marked (TPT) are from The Passion Translation®. Copyright © 2017, 2018, 2020 by Passion & Fire Ministries, Inc. Used by permission. All rights reserved. ThePassionTranslation.com.

Scripture taken from The Voice™. Copyright © 2012 by Ecclesia Bible Society. Used with permission. All rights reserved.

Editor: Krista Dunk

Interior Design: Dana Williams

Cover Design: Nadia Kahtria

Author photo: Joseph McCalment

First Edition, 2022

ISBN (pb): 979-8-218-08067-9

Publisher: Saphar Publishing

This book is dedicated to my amazing family:

Bruce, *thank you for believing in me and pushing me to write the message I have been carrying in my heart. Together, we have fought hard, persevered, and seen God provide many blessings. May God use our story to encourage and bring freedom for others.*

Ian, *your compassion, counsel, and care for others are God-given, and it makes my momma's heart proud. May God use those things to impact the world around you for generations to come as you commit your ways to Him.*

Aubry, *you are magnetic; people are drawn to the light of Christ that shines brightly from you, and you make this momma smile with such incredible joy. May your passion for life, exuberance, and love shine as bright as the stars, leading others to His glorious presence.*

Haley, *your sensitivity to God's heart and your love for truth is like a precious treasure, bringing such deep delight to my soul. May God continue to reveal mysteries to you as you mine the gold from others. You will point nations toward the kindness of the Father's heart.*

Mom and Dad, *thank you for fostering in me a passion for God's heart and voice. I appreciate your example of steadfastness through the storms and always reminding me I was chosen for a purpose. May this book not only reveal God's goodness but serve as part of my legacy and yours.*

CONTENTS

NOTE TO THE READER

Some would call me the girl next door. Most days I sport a simple ponytail and yoga pants, other days my favorite jeans. Whatever the uniform, I desire to tackle each day head-on in pursuit of purpose. Blending in with the crowd, I doubt anyone would see me as Indiana Joan or Laura Croft. There is a level of mystery that entices me though, and I am ready for adventure.

This book, and life in general, are part of a journey; it's my pilgrimage of sorts. The path before me is marked by adventure, curiosity, and the expectation that anything is possible if you have faith. I don't think this journey is mine alone; in fact, I would love for you to join me. Together we can look ahead at the roads, intersections, and chasms yet to be crossed. Though many of our steps will be about the physical world, we will see that the majority happen in the deep, unseen places in our hearts.

We could define this journey as the constant war between what our eyes see here on earth and what our hearts were created for. Our steps are not just about the end result or destination. Instead, the essential parts of the journey are happening in the moments of *everything in between*. From the earliest sign of life, our lives are marked with purpose. Then, from the moment we take our first breath, our hearts come alive with an insatiable desire to pursue more. That desire is an invitation that calls us onto the highways where anything is possible. Though the road is not always clear or easy, what He invites us into is exciting and allows for advancement or growth.

As a child, I felt the tug of war going on in my soul. Though sometimes subtle, I could sense the internal and external struggle between this world's reality and what God's reality was calling me toward. Contentment and longing coexisted. The longing wasn't because I had a bad home life. I have a great family. No, the tug in my soul wasn't about circumstances, but rather two worlds. It was a tug of war in my heart pulling me toward possibilities in God or back to limits due to my human condition.

Growing up in suburbia, I didn't have to fight through gangs to get to school, but I did have to stand tall against complacency, judgment, and perfectionism. In the middle of my normal childhood, I encountered Jesus. I felt His tangible love and experienced His Spirit living inside of me. It was more than an imaginary thought. I had confidence that God loved me, spoke to me, and had a plan for my life.

I didn't start this adventure because I have a high view of myself. Yes, I knew I was special to God, but I also had to fight against the thought that I wasn't *anything* special. Maybe you have had that thought too? There is a constant war raging between what God says and what the world says. External and internal battles war between ordinary and extraordinary.

Every day we have the option to take a path. One path has an upward wind and advances us toward the miracles God has waiting to show us. The other path is a downward slope that takes us in circles, acting as a snare into distraction, discouragement, or lack. In the chapters ahead, we will look at ways to push through the valleys (leaving behind limitations) and develop hope for new heights (pushing toward possibilities). We will ask hard questions and look at how everyday steps contain destiny. We will explore pursuit and permission so our hearts can be content and exhilarated at the same time.

I have lived in many U.S. cities and have traveled all over the globe. From experience, I can say that road trips and airplanes can take us on an adventure, but there is nothing as great as the adventure we can have walking with God toward possibilities. Our success on this journey depends on how we choose to navigate it all. We are invited into awareness, as we take note of how we walk when times are good and how we press through when challenges arise.

Though none of us have all the answers, we know the One who does. The same God who spoke stars into alignment and created us in our mother's womb is with us. He is asking us if we are ready for a ride; a ride that defies logic and limitations. Together we can do this – you, me, and Holy Spirit! We can face our fears, sharpen our communication skills, and lean into intentionality. No matter which mile marker we are at, our steps matter.

This journey is about drawing closer to His voice and heart. It is not just about moving ahead or at the correct times; it's about following His lead to the places He has prepared for us: to realms of abundance and promise. The path before us will move us away from disappointment and position us for possibility as we *go after more*! This requires us to position our eyes and posture our hearts, following the voice of the One who promises to walk with us. We will see that blessing come as we commit our ways to follow Him, embracing what is between the now and the not yet.

In the chapters ahead, we will figure out what it looks like to dive deeper into His love, go further into purpose, and rise higher in our thinking. As companions walking together, we can defy limits and go after more. Using lessons I have learned or am learning, we will go after knowing, trusting, and experiencing who God is and what He has called us into. The journey is about Him and is also about us. God is inviting us into awareness of our need for Him, then into purpose. Won't you join me? *Let's leave behind limitations, follow His voice and heart, and take this path towards possibilities!*

1

IS THIS IT?

LIFE IS MESSY. It can feel complicated, busy, and even a little mundane. I am sure you would agree that there are days when you have it all together and other days you just want to survive. As we see the culture shift and watch world events unfold, we wonder *have I changed or just the world around me?* We wake up every morning, serve our families, and work jobs to provide and make an impact. Our hope is that we leave things better than we found them.

In all honesty, walking through these last few years has given me a greater awareness of who I am and how I react to life. There has been a real struggle to navigate the external world of pandemics, political chaos, isolation, and job loss. Not to mention there have been internal struggles of loss, hormones, depression, and discouragement. You may agree that there is a struggle between living proactively and reactively. Have you felt it?

One of the greatest desires of any human is to be valued and to add value. Out of that comes a cry to live from a place of fullness, not depletion. No one hopes just to *survive*. We want to walk through life, adding value from a place of wholeness. It may not be the thing you wake up thinking about, but when you throw out the to-do lists, erase some of the appointments on your calendar, and finally get through the pile of laundry, you realize there are hopes, maybe even dreams left to pursue. Subconsciously, there is a thirst for more. Deep inside our souls, beyond the desire to see success in our daily choices, relationships, and circumstances, we long to understand and walk in fullness. There lies the tension between the comfort we live in and the possibilities out our front door.

Somedays, I dream of living off the grid and far away from the craziness of city life. This city girl grew up in various large cities across five different states from the central U.S. to the West Coast. Though I have spent my entire life in suburbia, there is a small part of me that's tempted to live outside of our fast-paced society of on-demand movies, doorstep deliveries, and drive-through coffee. I imagine that living away from those things, that feel like necessities, would change the way I live. Pondering the change in the externals makes me think it would also change the way my mind and heart respond.

Part of me can't imagine living without these comforts. The world we are surrounded by has conditioned us to expect things quickly. We build self-contained communities for convenience, and we flock to megastores where everything is accessible in one place. Don't throw this book! I am not saying those things are bad. Let me clarify; I am a massive fan of all things convenient. In fact, I love a good television show where someone is left to survive (off the grid on their own). I especially love to watch them as I am nestled in my blanket, sipping my coffee, with the air conditioning on! Yes, I love convenience. However, this mindset of quick gratification can fuel the fire of impatience and entitlement...if we allow it to.

Unfortunately, living in a world with complete access to everything hasn't made our culture happier. Research shows that society has more of everything except personal value, fullness, and joy. Although we can get anything we want in minutes, we feel more alone and emptier than generations before us. Why is this?

The hustle of life becomes our focus. We strive to make efficient use of our time to be the best employee, spouses, friends, and parents. We default to pride and affirmation on our temporary success and lose sight of what true fullness means. There is tension between living in the present and living to make the future moments count. Our hearts get satisfied with the immediate gratification from our newest online purchase, then we bury the more profound longing we have for the extraordinary. The focus on the urgent and essential has squelched the hunger and pursuit hiding inside us. We see the physical world, yet feel the tug inside us, saying *this can't be everything. Is this it? Could there be more?*

One day, elbow deep in a sink of suds, scrubbing the grime off of last night's dishes, a similar thought crossed my mind. *This world's routines and daily struggles can't be the only thing I am living for.* Don't get me wrong, our days are filled with things that matter, right? We work to provide for our family. Our to-do lists and tasks focus on their needs, serving them, and making our homes a haven for those we love. In the middle of all that, we haven't forgotten God. He matters. We even agree He deserves everything, and then we continue to live each day doing *all the things*. Yet, in the middle of the high demands and busy moments, we wonder if our lives truly make a difference. Are we spending our time doing valuable things or things depleting us of actual value?

In an effort to have external results and maximize our time, we have defaulted back to convenience. Our lives revolve around our ability to juggle and balance all the things so we can make the most *significant impact*. Our days become part of the grind until we realize we have unintentionally added weight and pressure to our already full plates. We *are* just surviving...loaded down with weights put on by ourselves and others. Ultimately, relying on a limited mindset keeps us from doing all the incredible things our hearts long to do.

Surrounded by dish soap and discouragement, my heart wasn't just focused on the cycle of daily chores or monotony. I acknowledged my desire to experience *more* in my life. I wept at that realization. I was juggling my responsibilities. I took care of all the important things. Some moments I even thought, *wow, I am crushing it!* But there was a longing in my soul that wasn't content with keeping things *as is.* Yes, I had a nice home, a great family, and important roles to fill at home and church, but there was something missing. My relationship with Jesus was thriving too, but within that, I knew there was still more.

Let's pause for a moment. Some of you are wondering, did I miss something? Isn't it good to balance it all? Shouldn't I make the most of my time? There is some wisdom in that, but focusing on external acts may keep us from looking at the internal aspects of our lives.

If we are going to look at life as a journey, we must first align ourselves with one essential truth: God sets eternity in our hearts (see Eccl 3:11). God's Word says He has placed the desire for destiny and eternity in the depths of our soul. He has built into our DNA the longing for *extraordinary* possibilities. We live on this earth, but heaven has already marked our hearts. Eternity is at the core of our design. We were created for eternity and given destiny. You might imagine destiny as being the place where you finish. However, destiny is about who we are created to be and how we walk through life, not just our destination.

Our everyday life is significant. Though we don't always see it, there are ways to matter and have influence in the middle of the monotony of dinners, deadlines, carpools, and chores. There once was a time when I bought into the idea that my life could not consist of much more than paying bills and caring for people. Have you had similar thoughts like, *maybe I could insert searching for happiness on the weekends...if I wasn't exhausted.*

Can I propose another thought? Maybe we don't have to limit our expectations or dreams. Maybe dreaming doesn't have to seem selfish or foolish. If we can push past external forces, expectations, and opinions, we might see validity in the idea that it's okay to go after more. If we realize we are on a journey that takes some time, then it's all right to acknowledge we have felt guilt and shame about asking the question, "Is this it?"

If you're like me, you might be squirming a little in your seat, thinking, *I have guilt and feel selfish about wanting more.* In the middle of our feelings, before we even try, we bring up the "should haves." You know, stuff like *I should have* attempted big things before family or careers. Or maybe we push off the impossible for another day saying, *someday, when I don't have (fill in the blank), I will be able to make a difference.* Then we push aside the wonder which also asks, "Is there more?"

There is no shame attached, and my heart is excited that we can add this to part of our journey. I have asked the same questions and believe they come from a soul in pursuit. Our hearts long for significance, purpose, and influence. We long to do life well without settling for *okay,* or even *good.* That is how we *should* define the journey we're on. We seek permission to keep our feet on the ground, living with intentionality, while allowing God to stir up the desire of our hearts to soar high above it all. There is a balance between contentment and contending and between rush and patience (more about this later).

In the middle of my kitchen, washing away remnants from a delicious meal, which most likely involved chicken nuggets, I realized I wasn't happy with a mediocre life. My natural eyesight started to bother me. Rubbing my eyes, I realized I was frustrated with more than the limitations of my prescription glasses; I wanted to see God clearly move in my life and show up for me in ways that are beyond what I can physically produce.

At that moment, I remembered a story I read about Jesus crossing paths with a blind man. The disciples assumed he was blind because he or his parents had sinned. Jesus put them in their place, explaining his blindness was not about sin; it was so that God could display goodness and possibility, instead of leaving him in limitation and lack. Then, Jesus spits in the dirt, makes a mud pie, and smears it on the man's eyes. Not quite the home remedy we expect, right? Give us a little bottle of oil maybe, but mud in the eye? (See John 9.)

Looking at the way Jesus handled this situation tells me Jesus doesn't always take the traditional approach to fix problems. Just read the Gospels! With mud on his face, knowing life is a mess and culture has already stereotyped him as a sinner, the blind man goes to wash off in the Pool of Siloam. "Go," Jesus told the man with the muddy face, and somehow the blind man (who can't see and is dripping mud all over the place) makes his way to the pool. Siloam means "sent." He had been sent to remove the limitations from his sight.

With this realization, tears filled my eyes and started spilling out onto my clean dishes. God's desire for us is to see clearly and know clearly that our natural circumstances don't have to be *as is*. Jesus could show up in our everyday life, while we are sitting on the street stuck in blindness, at work, in line at the grocery store, or doing dishes. Are we desperate enough to have Him rub mud over the problem to fix it? Are we ready to break free from the tension of our culture, an instant and urgent culture, yet one that is stuck in lack?

Do you see the process in this story? The disciples ask a question about *why* this man is blind, and it leads them to examine the man's life and family. After analyzing his childhood, the problem hasn't gone away; he is still blind. Jesus steps in, and He shows the blind man that *this isn't how it has to be*. There are other options! Then, He messes up the clean nature of their assessment. Mud everywhere, Jesus gives instructions and sends the man on a journey. Who knows how long it took the blind man to get there or how fast he traveled.

Our next-day deliveries and single-pod cups of coffee have us living in an urgent-important box. Our mindsets, beliefs, and focus hang out in the immediate. We are creatures of habit and comfort; the last thing we want is mud in our eyes. I get it! I am embarrassed to say that one day when my Keurig stopped working, I had a moment of panic. How would I get caffeinated and finish my list? The lack made me anxious to fix the problem. The solution wasn't as quick as hitting a button on my machine. Thankfully there was a pour-over dispenser hidden in the back of my cabinet, which reminded me that sometimes we must slow down and do things the unconventional way. Joy filled my heart when I finally poured the boiling water over the fresh grounds and listened to the drip of the new brew. Yes, I am being a little dramatic, but I do think there is something exceptional about a slow-drip cup of flavorful coffee. Just as I believe wholeness comes from the journey that can't be completed in a day.

If I follow a similar process as the blind man, I could reflect on my childhood and see I was a good kid. Growing up, I strove to be a good student, athlete, employee, and friend. My temperament then and now is steady, trustworthy, and not impulsive. Even as a teen, I was respectful, diligent, and didn't shy away from working hard. That being said, I did carry a label: my friends affectionately nicknamed me "Miss Perfect." That was part of my problem.

I lived with extreme internal pressure to live up to the label, and being my own worst critic caused me to live in a performance mentality driven by a deep desire to please people. My inner world demanding perfectionism brought on a lot of rejection. Constantly working to be the very best I could be, I didn't want to disappoint people or give God less than He deserved. There was a healthy fear of God mixed with a good relationship with Him. Both were accompanied by a desire not to mess it up! Reverence for the Lord is good, but I took "performance" too far. I was aware of my problems. The fear of rejection wasn't the only thing limiting me. Fear of failure trailed right behind it.

Yet, just as Jesus did for the blind man, Jesus spoke to my heart and said, "Go!" He sent me on a journey that would require faith and sometimes wise people to surround me, leading me through blind intersections (pun intended). The journey is not a quick one. In fact, I am still somewhere between the *go* and the *wholeness*. But God, in His faithfulness, is leading me around the mountains and accompanies me in the valleys to experience lessons that are best learned through time and effort. Navigating through friendships, education, the workplace, marriage, children, and ministry has given me many opportunities to understand my own limitations. As complex and challenging as it is, sojourning through life has given me skills that only come when I don't speed through it.

Whether out of desperation or being full of faith, I stood at the sink that day and committed to never being defined by limitations again. I knew Jesus was able to remove my limited sight (both natural and spiritual). With uncharacteristic impulse, I left the clean dishes on the counter and ran outside. On my knees in my backyard, I vowed to pursue possibilities. With determination, I reached for the hose, made some mud, and smeared it on my face. It was my *Braveheart* moment (or maybe I do have a little Laura Croft living inside somewhere). It was my vow to believe God to do impossible things and let Him restore sight in all areas of my life.

Life doesn't have to be *as is*. He has sent us, and we will journey. Through the pages of this book and beyond, we will take one step at a time away from the hustle and the comfortable. Slowly inching away from where we have been, we can separate ourselves from comparison, shame, and disappointment. Then, we will keep our eyes on the new path towards purpose and abundance.

As we begin our journey to go after more, let's discuss four critical components needed to navigate the highs and lows. With one foot in front of the other, we will look at how patience, attitude, encounters, and hunger are essential to living well on earth. Paying attention to the steps along our path helps make each moment matter while remembering one essential truth: we have been designed for eternity. Our hearts were created to explore possibilities and not live within limitations. Our very beings have been designed for more than our eyes can see and our minds can fathom. You and I have been made to pursue wholeness, remove labels, and let Jesus reveal solutions.

So, with the **PATH** in front of us, let's step out of the mundane towards a greater awareness of what destiny truly means for us now. It's time to encounter more in our circumstances and souls. Jesus says to you, "*Go, there is permission for more!*" Do you believe it?

God has built into our DNA the longing for
extraordinary possibilities.

Questions and Reflections
...to ponder on your way to possibilities!

➤What are the things in your life that you see as healthy?

➤What are some longings or dreams that have not been fulfilled?

➤What thing has been holding you back from those dreams?

➤What labels have limited you in the past?

➤What do you think it means for God to "plant eternity in our hearts" (Ecclesiastes 3:11)?

Part one

PATIENCE

2

WAITING

My husband and I were bliss-filled newlyweds, excited to start our life together and have a carload of kids. We dreamed of having four. On our one-year anniversary, we decided we wouldn't prevent them from joining us. However, after a few months, I got a little anxious. That is, when we moved from not preventing to actively trying. With no baby in sight, getting pregnant became our priority. (When I say that, I mean it became my greatest desire and ultimate focus.) We saw baby things everywhere, got invited to hundreds of baby showers, and wondered what we should name our children.

We dreamed, prayed together, and had friends praying for us. We enjoyed the season we were in, but we longed for more. Excitement built for the day when our couple's status would change to a family. We loved God and knew how much He loved us. Family is important to Him, so we lived our days believing He would make it happen. We were convinced our time was just around the corner, but with each day, we sat at the proverbial red light...waiting.

I researched, read books, and heeded any advice that might help. There were charts about certain foods to eat or avoid. I was willing to try almost anything. We did what we could, knowing ultimately it was out of our control. Looking back, I should have bought stock in pregnancy tests. Whenever I felt any type of pregnancy symptom, I took a test. Every month I was convinced I was pregnant. All the signs were there. Well, almost.

We loved being us and enjoyed our time together. But as they do, our emotions rose and fell like a rollercoaster. As each month passed, we felt hopeful and then disappointed. Holding onto hope was easy at first because we both believed God had promised us children. It never crossed our minds that He wouldn't. There were moments when hope felt more distant. When we don't see forward movement, we can feel defeated. The doctors had convinced us to let two years pass before running any tests, so we waited. The calendar's pages turned as we continued trying.

RED LIGHT MOMENTS

Sometimes moments make complete sense, and the next step seems logical. However, other times, like the one I just shared, make no sense at all. We were left confused and wondering what to do next. More than once, I realized how stuck I felt. It was as if I was at a red light, in the middle of the street, watching everyone else pass by. Yet, I hadn't been given permission to go. Others had been given their green light, and as expected, they took off while I was forced to sit.

Those seasons of waiting for the light to turn green are challenging. Let's get real; we tend to get antsy after just a few seconds of waiting! We panic, thinking about all the things we will miss out on. We can't take our minds off three pressing words: *how much longer?* Seconds turn into minutes, and we start to rationalize that the light sensor must be broken. We lose patience. Here I am, patiently waiting at this light for way too long. Our emotions and expectations tell us other people are living their best life, surrounded by their tribe. As we wait, we lose joy and feel like a victim stripped of permission.

Culture has told us that fulfillment only comes when forward movement is taking place. If momentum is not happening, we feel defeated.

This must be what a thoroughbred feels as it stands saddled, ready for the race to begin. I envision the jockey mounted, pulling back the reins, while the champion stirs restlessly in the holding gate. In anticipation, the horse's heart races, knowing it's almost time. Restless, he looks ahead for the gate to open, giving permission to run with wild abandonment.

Maybe you have been there or feel like that describes you right now. You are not alone. Many people feel like a barrier stands between them and their destiny. Like the thoroughbred, do you relate to being held back...waiting? If you can relate to this, you also understand how frustrating the red light can be. Rest assured; you are not alone! I think you need to hear that again. You are not the only person who has felt that way. It does not make you weak or strip you of value.

What I have learned (and find encouraging) is that red-light moments make the green lights even more meaningful. Our goal should be to see the meaning during the journey and realize it's not all about external movement. Though I didn't realize it until after, waiting helped me discover that what's happening inside is just as important. If we sort through the mundane parts of our busy days, we can find the remarkable moments we can launch from.

YOU ARE NOT ALONE

We cannot journey alone. If you are reading this book, I want you to see the value in joining with others to make it further. I love the idea of reaching one hand out to someone further down the road and our other hand out to someone coming up from where we have been. We must look for help along the way from others who have gone before us, making similar journeys, so we can help those behind us. Other people's triumphs and defeats become our life lessons. We can look at the fears faced and the joy they experienced. Let's get real. I'd much rather hear a story about someone who faced their struggles, and then finished strong!

Everyone loves a good hero story. Some of my favorite hero stories are in the Bible. The author of Hebrews lists men and women who had to overcome incredible obstacles (see Hebrews 11). The list is full of regular people who were mocked, faced disappointment, and were hunted down. They were people who learned how to defeat discouragement and escape death. The situations they faced were intense. And if you are like me, you want to figure out how they made it onto this MVP hero list!

Hero status seems like a high bar to reach, so those who truly deserve this title have accomplished major feats in their lives. One of those heroes of faith is mentioned in the Old and New Testaments. The Bible tells us Abraham was a man who believed in God's promises without fault. Hebrews tells us his faith opened a credit account of approval or rightness with God. For Abraham to achieve hero status, including the title of "friend of God," he must have lived an extraordinary life, right? One reason I love his story so much is because his ordinary failures led to extraordinary victories.

This hero started off as most do: ordinary. But after a long journey, Abram became Abraham! His journey required him to repeatedly move and to wait. In the process, he encountered insecurity, failure, heartbreaks, loss, and everything in between. He made mistakes like telling half-truths, being afraid of powerful people, fixing problems without God, and laughing when things didn't make sense. Like us, he encountered family drama, jealousy, loss, and brokenness. Do you see why I can relate to this man? This hero of faith is like us!

Though Abraham took shortcuts, encountered pitfalls, and made mistakes, he is mentioned as one who had great faith. I love what Hebrews says about him. It remembers him as one who, "after waiting patiently, received what was promised" (Hebrews 6:15 NIV). Abraham gives me great hope! If he could learn how to overcome despair in waiting for his promise to be fulfilled, so can I. So can you! His life gives us an idea of what a journey toward patience looks like. His story and mine showcase a few keys that will help us wait patiently in the red-light moments. Before we look at his red-light moment, we must first see Abraham's green light.

GREEN MEANS GO

Abraham loved God and was committed to listening for His voice. He didn't wake up one day and decide it was time to move! Instead, Abraham heard God's voice telling him to "Leave your country, your people, and your father's household, and go to the land I will show you." He was invited to step into his destiny.

Imagine walking 400 miles on foot! Talk about a long trip! Accompanied by his wife, nephew, and all he owned, Abraham packed the family wagon and began his quest toward great possibilities. Knowing that success and growth depended on obedience, God called them out of familiarity and into new places. This required leaving comfort and aligning their hearts to God's heart.

Life is full of moments and situations where we either choose to get comfortable or push out into the unfamiliar. I myself am a creature of habit. I have my coffee out on the back deck or go to the same coffee shop because there is something reassuring about knowing what to expect. Often, we default to the everyday, natural routines and rhythms that become our street of familiarity. We may enjoy the typical way we interact with our spouses, kids, co-workers, or neighbors. However, deep inside us, there is still a desire for something out of the ordinary. Like Abraham, we have the opportunity to leave familiarity on a path toward incredible promise. This journey toward the unknown, uncommon, or unpredictable opens us up to possibility.

Are you starting to feel it? Do you sense the tug toward promise? A well-taken journey requires us to pack our bags, step off the curb of complacency, and begin to advance. Leaving the sidewalk of safety sets our journey in motion. After all, can we grab ahold of the new if our hand is clenched, holding onto the old? Abraham had to let go of his past to find his future. With no timeframe or specifics, God said, "Go." Some of you are starting to bite your nails, but I assure you getting a vision for your hopes and dreams does not come by looking behind or down. Expectation requires risk, which sounds like an adventure to me!

I propose that the gaze from Abraham's curb was grand. He was given promises, God-sized ones. God assured him that he would become, "a great nation, and I will bless you; I will bless those who bless you, and whoever curses you I will curse, and all the peoples on earth will be blessed through you" (Genesis 12:2-3 NIV). That may seem outlandish to a man without an heir or clear purpose, but I believe they pierced Abraham at his core. Those promises ignited dreams and a desire that would move him into destiny.

God took this homeless wanderer and set him on a path of epic adventure. God promised Abraham the land of his enemies, protection, and provision, but specifically, he was assured fatherhood. Without seeing it right in front of him, he looked heavenward as God showed him the stars, saying his children would be as many as the bright lights. What a promise!

When we hear a promise, we naturally get excited for it to happen. What if we heard a promise like Abraham's? *Wow, God, that's amazing! I can't wait to be a dad (or a mom). Let's get the baby's room ready!* Then, we expect the answer to come quickly, right? Doesn't God give us a promise, and then rush to fulfill His Word? After all, He is faithful, loving, and able. I am sure Abraham heard God speak and couldn't wait for it to happen the following month. Little did Abraham know he was about to encounter a long red light and sit there for decades!

Remember when I said I could relate to much of Abraham's journey? I, too, was confident God had given me a promise. He spoke to my heart, assuring me I would have children. I didn't know what the timeline would be, but I had faith. In the meantime, I was working a job that I didn't like. Every day, I forced myself to get up and go to work, keenly aware I was not living my best life. I knew I was created to have a family and add value in other ways. So, what did I do? I quit my job! Yes, I called my husband from work, crying uncontrollably, and told him I couldn't do it anymore. Thankfully, he understood. That is when I decided to step out of familiarity. Sure, I didn't love the familiar job, but I still was stepping into unknown waters. From that place, I was hopeful that two things awaited: piano students and motherhood.

I was not pregnant, but in the waiting, I moved forward. I was determined not to get complacent while waiting. After a few home improvement projects, I knew it was time to add a few piano students to my routine. One thing I learned (and taught my students) is that timing is everything. We can't go by feelings, and we can't do things our way. The song's composer had a vision and left us instructions. Now, we are responsible to remain steady and on tempo. To do this, we used a device called a metronome which helps with speed and consistency. The clicking sound it produces shows us how fast or slow we should play a song. If we align our movement to the beats per minute, we can move at the right tempo, not at our own pace.

TIMING IS EVERYTHING

Just as in music, there is a stop-and-go rhythm to our journey. Obedience and patience is required for the flow. The tension we feel between complacency and contentment could cause us to speed up or slow down. It could cause us to lose consistency in the going or in the waiting. There is a rhythm we must find in the process. Instead of seeing movement as success, what if we saw the rhythm of our heart aligning with God's rhythm as success?

Here is how we *go and wait* well. It is measured by the tempo of our hearts. The atmosphere of what is going on inside of us can determine how fast we move or how well we wait. Our heartbeat beats faster when anxious thoughts come. It creates an uneasiness in our bodies which makes it harder to stay still. We feel the need and impulse to move or speed up our timeline. When we are completely relaxed, our heart beats at a slower pace and the tempo of our drive diminishes, which could cause us to fall behind.

God sees our path and knows what He is doing in those deep places of our hearts. He understands the fears and insecurities that make us want to jump ahead of the click of His timing. He also places a rest symbol in the music of our life to tell us a pause is needed. Those red-light moments create space and prepare us for what He is bringing our way.

Are you in the waiting? I want to encourage you that there is work being done on the inside. The pause's momentum, movement, and maturing are just as significant as the external travel. In fact, it is actually more important. If this is true, and I believe it is, ask yourself what areas of your life have stopped. Where does your life seem to be stalled? What aspects of your marriage, family, finances, or ministry have you paused, waiting for a clear sign to keep going? You might feel it internally; your emotions may need a chance to mature, refresh, or be figured out. Maybe you are waiting for external movement, like a promotion or acknowledgment to come from a boss or leader. I understand where you are. It is not easy to be longing for more but unable to get it.

Timing is everything. My moments at home, teaching piano, but longing to be a mom, were like that thoroughbred waiting for the gate to open. Your moments might feel much the same, but although you are stopped, it doesn't mean the green light isn't ahead. If God has promised you what you cannot see yet, do not fear! Hold onto hope for that thing He has promised, that thing you have a deep desire for. Just like Abraham looked to the sky to count the stars, we can look to the heavens and know that what God has promised He will perform.

In the chapters ahead, we will look at ways patience will help us along this journey toward possibility.

⁓

A well-taken journey requires us to pack our bags,
step off the curb of complacency,
and begin to advance.

Questions and Reflections
...to ponder on your way to possibilities!

➤Do you identify in some way with feeling held back or limited by something or someone?

➤What area of your life feels paused or stalled?

➤What do you think about the following statement? "Red-light moments make the green lights even more meaningful."

➤If a "well-taken journey requires us to pack our bags and step off the curb of complacency," then what areas of your life could be described as complacent?

➤What is one promise you feel that God has given you? (Either through a verse in the Bible or spoken to your heart.)

3

WONDERING

Was something wrong? Waiting led to wondering, and our reality of trying for a child became filled with doctor's appointments... way too many visits. Each appointment included tests, prodding, pictures, machines, and hours of wondering. We tried to hold onto faith, but other emotions and beliefs slowly shoved their way into the picture. Soon, worry and fear were mixed with our faith. Stress joined the waiting too, and all the feelings were there. In that place, we sat wondering when God would do what He said. We asked what we could have done differently and tried to make sense of the lack.

Wondering is a mind game. This hypothetical game is won or lost in our thoughts and expectations. *What if* thoughts consume our mind and get rooted in our imagination, causing the wondering thoughts to either be self-defeating or full of hope. The outcome is defined by our choice of thoughts. What are you wondering about? Are you wondering why you *haven't* (fill in the blank) or *aren't* (fill in the blank)? Are you wondering why you *don't* or *can't*? Are you running through the list of what-ifs? The negative approach to wondering can lead us down roads we don't want to travel. Those roads lead to anxiety and worry, which cradles us in fear.

After months of not knowing *why* we couldn't get pregnant, an answer finally came. Somehow, my husband was given a free vasectomy because of an injury or defect from birth. *How convenient.* Not really! Our hearts sank. We sat, cried, and processed the news. We needed that pause to re-group and talk through the pain. Finally, with the report, we had some answers and a choice. In front of us was the opportunity to decide what path we would follow.

We didn't believe it was the end of our story, and we were praying it wasn't the end of hope. Were we discouraged? Yes, there were moments of discouragement and emotions like anger and self-pity. With that many emotions, thoughts tried to convince me God had abandoned us or that we were facing this disappointment alone. When those thoughts came, I pushed them away. I couldn't agree with them, because although I was sad, I knew I was not alone or forgotten. My heart went through the grief and disappointment of what I thought my life would look like. Worry tried to accompany my wonder, but then I knew it was time to take a step off the curb of familiarity and keep pressing on towards our promise. The question was, how would we do that?

WORRY INTO WORSHIP

I appreciate facts; knowing and having things figured out feels safe, and the very definition of *wonder* can signify doubt and uncertainty. There are things we will have to process or think about before we have answers. That is one side to the word *wonder*. The other aspect of wonder is excitement, astonishment, and amazed admiration.[1] Our time of wondering has two options: partner with worry or choose to stir up the awestruck admiration of the One who gave us the promise. We get to decide. Part of our journey is determining how we will navigate the challenging moments. Will we continue to feel stuck? Or leap over our limitations?

Worship is crucial for a heart that wants to know God and develop a clearer picture of who we are. Worship is about value. We worship what we see as valuable, and from a place of worshiping a wonderful King, we also find our value. Worship is not just for the One to be worshiped. It is also for the heart that's giving adoration and praise. Worship exalts the answer higher than our questions. Worship releases our worries and fears from their grip on our hearts; it hands them over to a King who is worthy and able to change our path's course. Worship positions our hearts toward promise and away from worry. It focuses our hearts on the One who is supremely greater than every problem, obstacle, and heartache. No matter how big our problem is or how long the disappointment lingers, worship creates space to exalt God in our circumstances and confusion. It is a way to wonder, meaning to admire God.

A heart of worship puts faith, trust, and hope in God's ability. With every word or breath of worship, faith is stirred up. Disappointment, anger, fear, and worry are pushed out because there is no room for them to stand beside a mighty King. They have no place in our hearts if we allow our hearts to be full of His majesty, power, and glory. In those moments, we can take the *whys* and *what ifs* and exchange them for worship. We can unload worry so our hands can be lifted high to a God worthy of all our praise.

So, in my wonder, I chose to worship. In the place of being unable to produce a child, we decided to exalt God's plan, His goodness. We redirected our attention off our circumstances and to His goodness. During this time, I was encouraged to rejoice and worship. I love how the Contemporary English Version Bible talks about the barren woman's worship. It says, "Sing and shout, even though you have never had children! The LORD has promised that you will have more children than someone married for a long time" (Isaiah 54 CEV).

As I worshipped consistently through disappointment, hope rose in me. God tenderly reminded my heart of His goodness and the promise He had spoken. The circumstances said no, but God's promises began to beat wildly in my chest. I was confident that the same God who told Abraham to leave the familiar and step into the unknown was with us in our unfamiliar territory. With awareness of the problem, and then God's goodness, my heart felt the gentle reminder that God is faithful. I felt comfort and peace, just as Abraham had when God promised protection, provision, and a promised one. I'm sure Sarah and Abraham had moments like mine where they had to choose worship in the wondering.

Desperate times develop destiny. When we find ourselves walking a path and getting stuck in a moment of disappointment, we can lean into His promises by worshiping Him and reminding ourselves of what He said He would do! Worship strengthens us for the next steps. It creates space in our heart and circumstance for God to pour out His grace and strength. In addition to that, it enables us to exchange our worry and weakness for admiration and wonder. He is a mighty God who loves to direct us through impossible situations by showing us who He is and who we can become.

Remember, wondering is a mind game, but it's also an opportunity for our mind and heart to refocus on the One above it all. When we direct our attention and affection on His goodness, it does something remarkable: it shifts things! Our choice to worship with the right kind of wonder (amazed admiration) instead of wonder laced with doubt allowed things to shift. One day we were discouraged, but in the next moment, our hearts experienced revitalized hope. It was not because our circumstances had changed. Instead, our internal world was invited forward, away from feeling stuck. God began to direct our steps past another curb toward the open door. One promise I carried with me and still cling to today is from the book of Proverbs. Solomon's wise words remind my heart that I can plan my course, but it is "the Lord that directs my steps" (Proverbs 16:9 NIV).

Are there areas in your life that God is recalling, even at this moment? Are there circumstances that feel too big? Are you wondering *how?* Are you stuck in the *why?* There is One who deserves our praise, even in the moments when we don't understand. When there is doubt and uncertainty, we can turn our wonder into worship! How do we do this? We can find truth to believe about who

God is. Who has He been for you? Who does He say he is? What one thing can you mentally and emotionally shift your attention and affection toward? Identify and believe the truth, which exalts God above problems, and then watch what happens next!

PROVISION FOR PROMISE

One major lesson I learned by reading Abraham's story and walking through my own is that with every promise comes provision. Sometimes the answer is not what you expect, but it does come! We had not given up, and we knew God's answer (provision) was just a few days and one doctor away. With some open doors, the path toward promises and possibilities had been restored. Finally, we had a new level of hope to match the level of our faith. Not only was provision attached to God's promises, but new possibilities were present. God was providing and opening opportunities. We prayed through all the options, like adoption or seeking help with infertility. As we worshiped, listened, and followed the provision we saw, the path became apparent, and three simple letters began to point us toward our promise fulfilled: IVF (In Vitro Fertilization).

We were journeying through new territory. Neither of us had ever been through these endless procedures. We were in an unknown land, but as partners, my husband and I were invested in all that would be necessary. Our new reality became a land of doctors, nurses, fertility clinic visits, shots, blood draws, tears, bruises, swelling, and pain. Did I mention pain? I had never felt more like a pincushion than I did those weeks. Although the vasectomy was my husband's, we both had to undergo months of preparation and procedures to prepare our bodies for children. The pain was both physically and emotionally intense. Though the process seemed daunting, God's reminders of His faithfulness and goodness are never-ending.

During those moments, we were physically in constant movement. I spent hours driving to the clinic, only to be told that progress was being made. However, it still seemed like additional red lights.

When your eyes are fixed on the end destination, in our case having a child, the process can seem overwhelming. It is possible to be hopeful but still feel overwhelmed because there is no physical manifestation of that result. Progress? Progress felt like only reassuring words. Our circumstances had not yet changed; we were still childless.

Process is crucial as we follow God's heart and voice. Just as we saw in Chapter 2, aligning our heart to God's timing is necessary, especially if we want to develop patience. Process must happen before the product, and it was the same for Sarah and Abraham. They experienced many years of trying, waiting, expecting, hoping, and not seeing the fulfillment of the promise. Years passed and their bodies were past the age of possibility. In fact, they were caught laughing at God's promise. After so many years of waiting, the possibility of having a child was quite improbable. There could be no way, right? Never mind the Bible reminds us that all things are possible. That couldn't possibly apply to all situations. You probably think God couldn't have meant your home life, family, or finances, right?

Journeys don't happen overnight, and red lights can feel like an eternity. Trust me, ours had, and after years of trying to achieve our goal, we were still sitting at the same red light. Although we were close enough to see the possibility, there was still no physical fulfillment. We sat there with a new, revitalized feeling of hope, but we were still waiting, wondering, and wanting. We walked through two years of trying and many months of options, decisions, and IVF preparation.

Then, God spoke. When God affirms your attention or affections, it is time to take note! My Heavenly Father gently whispered to my heart, *"PATIENCE, child."* It was loving and timely. I needed to know that my heart's desire was not forgotten or misplaced. I needed to know God was with me, and I can reassure you that He is with you in the process. We are not forgotten. He doesn't leave us to navigate the hard moments alone.

His voice continued to speak to my heart, *"You have fought hard during this long season, and even when your eyes couldn't see the fulfillment, you maintained faith in difficult circumstances. I am so pleased with you. Patience. You are almost there."* Tears spring into my eyes even now as I think of those words that He spoke to my heart. I felt the welling up of love and the gentle assurance. God is a good Father who knows how to walk with us through challenging moments. He knows what we need to hear in the waiting. His loving voice reminds us we are set on a course toward a promise, and His provision goes with us every step of the way.

Not only had He made a promise, but He was also promising. It was active and daily. God doesn't just tell us to leave behind the familiar and fend for ourselves. Instead, He stays with us in the process. Why? Because He is in the business of fulfilling His Word. "He will never leave you . . . Do not be discouraged" (Deut. 31:8). I didn't need to give up believing; I just had to keep my heart still. Waiting had given me time to focus on His voice, especially when my emotions were raging.

I encourage you that the times that require us to sit, trust, and wait, are opportunities. They are full of moments for us to connect with His truth, ask questions, worship, and discover answers to deep-rooted uncertainties we *wonder about,* such as who God is for those He loves. Those red-light moments were all those things for me in my situation. They can be those things for you too. Those opportunities prepare us for what we are stepping into.

God not only provides promise and provision, but He helps us hold onto victory. Those who follow His voice find that "He guards the course of the just and protects the way of his faithful ones. Then you will understand what is right, just, and fair- every good path" (Proverbs 2:7-9 NIV). He led us down good paths. They were not easy paths, but they were full of promise and hope. God provided finances for the procedures and family to support us emotionally. God led us to an incredible doctor and team who walked with us through months of blood draws, medicines, hormonal lows, and physical pain. Provision accompanied the promise, and my husband and I were full of faith that we would see God fulfill His Word.

One day, after years of process, we took another pregnancy test. This time it told a different story. It now confirmed the truth we had hoped for. Finally, after multitudes of prayers and months of grueling procedures, we were pregnant. Our hearts leaped for joy, knowing we would hold what had been promised. Fast forward through nine months of pregnancy, my husband and I welcomed a perfectly healthy son into our family. Every finger, toe, and smile became an inheritance for two people who had waited, hoped, prayed, and believed.

THE BLESSINGS OF WAITING

Along the way, the process holds many small and large miracles. We did, and we would continue to fight for more. Like us, you have had victories, small or large in your own life. Maybe you have seen God show up for you in a practical way, like providing food or finances when you needed it most. Maybe you have seen Him provide physical or emotional healing. Through those experiences, we have an opportunity to cling to promises, watch for God's provision, and turn our worry into worship. I am sure you are not content to stop with one victory. I am not! The principles we learn from our experience can be applied to future situations, giving us the opportunity to see God do more in us and through us. After all, we are going after more!

A year after we held our newborn son, my husband and I chose to keep pursuing promises. By that, I mean we began another round of IVF preparation, which included similar emotions, pain, and hope. During that time, we revisited the lessons we learned, expecting we would navigate it even better the second time. We clung to our promise and fought for victory so we could add to our blessing. The miracles seen through that process will be saved for another time; they are too numerous to share here. Except to say, we received a double portion for all the years of turmoil and lack. We saw God show up for us in our desperate moments. When we felt disappointment, we praised it out of our thinking and fixed our hearts on declaring destiny. Our double portion arrived 20 months later when twin girls joined their big brother. Those tiny bundles were just as perfect, beautiful, and every bit as precious. We have an incredible inheritance!

In what way has your journey taken you through waiting and wondering? Do you relate to disappointment after disappointment? What promises would you like to see fulfilled in your job, kids, marriage, or ministry? Whatever is stirring in your heart, don't stop fighting for it. Though patience is required, use the moments to draw close to God and see His hand work internally, even before the external situations shift.

The process was long but so worth it. When I sat holding three precious littles, all under the age of two, my arms and heart were full. Inheritance can be defined by these three. Patience was required to get to this moment, and I am sure you can imagine patience would be needed to parent and love them well. The journey didn't stop, and problems didn't cease. Although I am not an expert on patience, let me remind you that trips are short, but our life journey unravels lesson after lesson. Each step, struggle, failure, and achievement deepens our insight into who we are (our identity) and who God is in the middle of it all. This gives us confidence that God's promises *are* worth going after no matter what life looks like. Our hearts *are* made to hear His voice and pursue His heart.

In our quest to know if there is more to our life than simply working to pay bills and surviving, God allows us to step off the curb into possibilities. He longs for us to make our way toward promise, stepping into the development of destiny. When God speaks, He will perform. His faithfulness walks with us, whispers to us, and withstands time.

The path away from limitations, disappointment, and distractions requires patience. Every step we take toward more must be saturated with patience. Because of this, God's words echo in my thoughts, and there were days when I couldn't get it off my mind. I found myself dialoguing with God constantly about this incredible word. In the hard moments, I found myself whispering, "I need more patience. Help me."

In a world of hurry, frustration, and uncertainty, that cry has not diminished. God continued to suggest not-so-subtle reminders of my need to dive deeper into patience. Every trying situation, red flag, or red-light moment allowed me to evaluate and dialogue with God. Here is what I am learning: red lights are about wonder. We can question God or ask questions from a heart of amazed admiration. In the process, we must pursue patience and ask God, "What more should I know about patience?"

Will we partner with worry or <u>choose to stir up the awestruck</u> <u>admiration</u> of the One who gave us the promise.

Questions and Reflections
...to ponder on your way to possibilities!

❧

➤Do you relate more to the definition of wonder as curiosity or awe?

➤What area of your life needs you to choose worship instead of worry?

➤What truth can you believe that will exalt God above your situation?

➤How do you feel about the following statement? "He knows what we need to hear in the waiting. His loving voice reminds us we are set on a course toward a promise, and His provision goes with us every step of the way."

➤In what ways (right now) have you set yourself up to "hear His voice and pursue His heart"?

4

PAY ATTENTION

THIS LIFE JOURNEY MATTERS. Every step can be a choice or an opportunity to advance toward something, learning more about God's nature, our nature, and how to value them both. I like to ask God simple questions. I truly believe prayer must be a dialogue. So, I often have a conversation, ponder those thoughts, and write them in a journal. Then, I wait for God's voice to respond. He is all about relationships, so when I ask, He responds. That simple question often brings about a gentle reply. One day, as I was asking Him to speak to me about where I was at in the process, God gently dropped words into my mind as if they were my thoughts. His voice often sounds like that. Yet, I have learned when thoughts come that sound more like His voice than my own, they are often God's.

The next thought could not have been my own. It came from thin air and wasn't related to anything I was thinking about. Although these words were not entirely outside my natural processing, I knew this voice. I had heard Him speak before; it was the voice of my Heavenly Father. After asking what I needed to see, He immediately stated, "Pay attention." He said it so matter of fact, yet with a hint of mystery. As I drove down the road, having this spontaneous conversation with God, I started to get annoyed. I had asked a question hoping for a discussion and some insight. I wanted more details, not two quick words.

After a moment of frustration, I responded to God, *I am! I am paying attention. I heard the promptings, and I am listening to You, God. What do You want me to know or see?* Then, I heard His sweet, kind, gentle voice again say, *pay attention*. However, I listened more carefully that time, and as He spoke those words, I heard Him enunciate the word differently. "Pay atten-*shunt*." Out of the word attention came the word *shunt*. It was a hint and enticement to pursue and ask more questions. It was an invitation into more than an answer. It was an invitation into a revelation! These are the moments we need to embrace as we go after more.

Inquisitively, I started wondering if patience was somehow related to paying attention. That question led me to ask more questions. For instance, *how does this connect to a shunt? What is a shunt? Why would this be the word that comes to mind?* This internal dialogue is taking place while I was still driving. Even though I had heard the term before regarding medical issues, I still didn't know much about it. My mind was reeling, and it took everything in me to keep driving instead of pulling over to Google the meaning. I decided to pay attention to the road and wait until I arrived home. Yes, even at that moment I had to choose patience.

The word shunt is defined by Webster's Dictionary as "to turn off to one side, shift; to switch from one track to another, divert; to bypass." The medical definition of a shunt (as a noun) is "a hole or small passage which moves, or allows movement of fluid from one part of the body to another."[2] Essentially, a shunt enables movement, which can look like the process of something turning aside or moving to an alternate course. We see this in medicine when a new passageway opens to allow fluid movement (as in channels of the heart). This term can also be used regarding electricity when a shunt device allows electric current to pass down an alternate path. The shunt creates a low resistance path for the current.

After reading the definition, the meaning struck a chord in my heart. A shunt is used surgically and practically to divert or permit flow from one pathway or region to another. There it was ..the meaning I was longing to understand. Patience allows us to lower resistance to the force and choose to turn and redirect our steps. It is the vehicle that diverts us from one pathway to another. It helps us make a shift, to change course, from a life of frustration to one of fruitfulness.

Plain and straightforward, patience allows a stillness of soul – a waiting – which enables us to stop and take inventory. The book of Proverbs explains it this way, "Pay attention to all that I have to say. Fill your thoughts with my words until they penetrate deep into your spirit. Then, as you unwrap my words, they will impart true life and radiant health into the very core of your being" (Proverbs 4:20-21 TPT). Those moments allow us to redirect our focus. It takes the focus off the circumstance and onto God's words, which affect our response.

In patience, we have permission to stop and redirect our thoughts, feelings, emotions, and attention. We can move away from anxiety and towards a calm thankfulness. Patience can be the shunt that redirects fear to the path of peace. Partnering with that moment, we can divert anger into understanding or compassion. Patience helps shift natural default actions toward choices that are good and life-giving.

Patience leads us on a path away from frustration and toward fruitfulness. God is good at confirming the words He speaks to my heart. Not long after marinating in this concept, I heard someone say that your pause can lead you to your field. How profound. A break is necessary for forward momentum. In the waiting, even in the stopping, God is getting us closer to our promise. Every pause we take opens a choice to stay on the current path or be redirected. In those moments, we receive a chance to grow in patience, choose misdirection, live in frustration, or be directed to fruitfulness. Those opportunities move us toward our promise! Patience opens a door into the more that is waiting for us. Patience propels us forward.

GET READY

How can patience propel you forward when it feels like it keeps us stuck in one place? Can I propose to you that patience is a temporary hold, not a definitive *no*. I believe the lesson God gave me that day was to say that these moments of alertness are an expectation to *get ready*! Yes, vigilance allows us to stay safe and avoid harm, but it also motivates us to get on the edge of our seats because something exciting is about to happen. We can quiet our hearts and alert all of our senses. There is an invitation to look more intentionally, listen with sharpness, and begin to understand things differently. It is an invitation to learn how to navigate our relationship with God and prepare ourselves for what He wants to do in us.

Whether Latin, Hebrew, Greek, or English, the definition of patience explains that endurance is required in our thinking and actions toward circumstances. It is the ability to calmly endure suffering or difficult situations. This self-restraint before activity looks like a power that is harnessed. It is a picture of a woman laboring in turmoil before the birth of the baby. We must calm the urge to make things happen before it's time. Instead, we must cling to hope, stay ready, and wait for the green light.

Patience does its work in us and it also works things out of us. That pause helps us acquire the grit needed for the journey. It gives us space to still our hearts before the Lord and wait on Him. God won't waste time. Instead, He gives us space to secure or anchor our hope in His promises. It gives us time to see God's actions in our circumstances and what is taking place in the spiritual realm.

Did you know there is a spiritual dimension that we can be part of every day? We live with our feet on the ground, but also in an unseen reality. We will spend more time on this later in the book. For now, I want to introduce you to a man who knew this principle well.

Ezekiel was born in ancient Israel during a time of division; the country was in turmoil. As a young man exiled from his land, he lived his life loving a God who created him to make a difference in his generation.

Ezekiel lived in a time of conflict, knowing despair, but surviving on hope. He heard God's voice and had the incredible ability to see into the spiritual realm. Eyes wide open, he walked through life staying aware of the different ways God would speak to His people. Ezekiel could see angels, saw visions of entire valleys of death corpses waking up and coming to life. This man who was already used to seeing and staying alert was given instruction from God to pay attention!

Ezekiel sees his homeland of Israel in a vision. Standing high on a mountain, he must catch his breath when a man of bronze appears in front of the gateway. I can only imagine the apprehension mixed with excitement in Ezekiel's heart. This supernatural encounter was probably not what Ezekiel anticipated that morning. However, the man of bronze spoke to Ezekiel, telling him to "look with (his) eyes and hear with (his) ears and pay attention" (Ezekiel 40:3-4 NIV). This angel appeared to give insight into what is to come. It was an invitation into wisdom and positioning to get ready!

I have seen angels and have had visions. There are two worlds we have access to. There are many keys to navigating these worlds, and we will discuss them throughout our time together. But first, I can assure you that you *are* created to navigate them. You can hear God speak and see with the eyes of your imagination if you start to pay attention. Ezekiel was given insight through his senses into what God was about to do. He had been in exile for 25 years before this vision of going back into his land. Undoubtedly, those years of exile were a struggle. I am sure he felt the turmoil, the twisting, the longing to get back what had been theirs. Ezekiel desired to see those things, but God didn't allow him to see that vision right away. There was a period of patience first that prepared him to see and get ready before the promise was fulfilled.

Ezekiel, Abraham, and each one of us has a choice to wait patiently for the right time or try to do things our own way. There is a reward for those who choose to harness the power God has placed inside of each of us. We might have to sit in turmoil for a time, but it is preparation for what is coming. As we anchor our hope to His promise, we can have confidence that "those who hope in (wait on) the Lord will inherit the land" (Proverbs 37:9 NIV).

Inheritance is promised. It was promised to Abraham when God said his descendants would be as numerous as the stars in the sky, and He promised it to us. The multiplication that Abraham experienced after waiting and wondering is available to us. Our path and destiny often require a time of preparation. But God is good, and when it's time, He shows up which makes it feel like a sudden move and multiplication. After all, I went from no kids to three in two years – even receiving twins! What type of multiplication have you already received or could you receive? What is in your heart right now? Are there dreams churning inside of you and coming to the surface as you read this? Pause and let your heart dream.

God longs to see you "passionately advance until the end [when] you find your hope fulfilled" (Hebrews 6:11 TPT). He wants to bring increase (multiplication) into your circumstances and repair the division in your relationships, businesses, finances, and dreams. He wants to divert you from frustration to fruitfulness, and all He is asking is that you pay attention. By saying those words, He is asking for our hearts.

Have you stopped giving Him your heart in the process? Have you found yourself caught in the trap of disappointment? Maybe you have given up fighting for your promises or forgotten what they are. What has He said? What does His Word say about who you are? What does the Bible tell us we have a right to?

If you think you have never heard Him speak to your heart before, don't fret. This journey we go on will sharpen your hearing and provide space to experience His gentle whispers that direct your path. The gentle tug you call conviction or conscience is where He speaks. If you have encountered that nudge of *I shouldn't do this*, or *get ready for more*, then you *have* heard His voice! You can hone those listening skills. Give Him your heart and pay attention, for His first promise is that He is about to do something new. God is all about taking us into new and glorious things.

Abraham and the heroes of faith learned to have confidence in what they hoped for and have assurance (a belief) in things we can't always see with our natural eyes. This pursuit, a walk of faith, requires us to stop, wait, and press forward, as we are encouraged again and again to pay attention and not give up!

We don't have to do this alone. You are not alone; get ready, because the way you see your path and life is about to change. Get ready! You might need to assess the emotions and condition of your heart so in the waiting you, "Don't allow your hearts to grow dull or lose enthusiasm but follow the example of those who fully received what God has promised" (Hebrews 6:12 TPT). Together, we will look at our lives and those who have gone before us. We will see how faith and patient endurance diverts us to the right path to receive an inheritance of life and abundance.

Whether you are at a red light now or find yourself there down the road, patience must become part of our DNA. We must realize we can either get caught in the discontentment trap or find success in waiting. Patience teaches us to bypass discontentment during our journey and be content in it all. Dissatisfaction shows who our hearts belong to and where our trust lies. Our actions either prove we trust in God to provide for the promise and fulfill His Word, or it shows we don't believe God will do what He says. We can choose patience and allow the process to have its complete work in us, allowing us to navigate both natural and spiritual realities.

If destiny is found only in the destination, how or why we journey doesn't matter. If we only count success as making it to a destination, then we lose the value and growth in the patient endurance and power we've harnessed. Destiny, our identity, and purpose are found in every step, not at the end of our life, otherwise our everyday activities would be meaningless. But they are not!

As we embrace destiny in the waiting, in the pressing forward, and in the moments in between, we can see inheriting the promise is part of all those moments. So, we must learn to pay attention. God is faithful to stop, redirect, and work in us. As we bypass discontentment, discouragement, and disappointment, we can press on toward inheritance. The question you might be asking is, what does pressing on toward inheritance look like? Can I tell you a little secret? It is all about following the signs!

Patience opens a door into the more that is waiting for us.
Patience propels us forward.

Questions and Reflections
...to ponder on your way to possibilities!

➤After reading the following verse, what is God saying to you? "Pay attention to all that I have to say. Fill your thoughts with my words until they penetrate deep into your spirit. Then, as you unwrap my words, they will impart true life and radiant health into the very core of your being" (Proverbs 4:20-21 TPT).

➤What is the thing you want to be directed away from, and what is the thing you want to be directed toward?

➤What do you think about the following statement? "Patience opens a door into the *more* that is waiting for us."

➤ What does God's Word say about who you are? What does the Bible tell us we have a right to?

➤If "destiny, our identity, and purpose are found in every step, not at the end of our life," then what is the one thing you are going to do today that is full of value and purpose?

5

DID I MISS IT?

HOW DID I miss the signs? That was my thought as I sat hunched over on my knees scrubbing the floor and wetting them with my tears. I felt a little like Cinderella. I had lost my prince charming and the only way I knew to make sense of the situation was to clean my bathroom floor while I wept.

It happened so subtly. I thought I had been paying attention, but somehow, I missed the depth of it. Guilt, anger, and betrayal were a few emotions raging in me. There was deep sorrow and compassion as well. I knew he didn't mean to get caught up in it all, but here we were.

Let me backup for a minute. Migraines were coming more often and disrupting our lives. My husband had them regularly since he was a teenager. I knew him then, and they came with stress, excitement, lack of sleep, and other triggers. Yet, he continued to fight through them, even in our early years of marriage. We sought medical help from every type of doctor imaginable. We believed for miracles and prayed for healing, knowing God was able and willing. But they kept coming.

Chronic pain takes on a life of its own. It is a constant battle, and the more headaches he had, the more I felt like a single mom raising three toddlers. I knew my husband loved us, and he was doing his best to keep his job and bring home a paycheck. Out of duty to provide for his family, he kept his job, but the rest was on me. I felt the weight of it becoming more and more strenuous every day. Yet, I loved being at home with my kids. Being a stay-at-home mom was a gift. I could raise little people who loved God and learned to hear His voice.

So, how did we end up here? He seemed to be sick on weekends, seeking solace in his room, laying in the dark when he wasn't at work because he was in pain. Come to find out, the doctors had prescribed more and more painkillers. In an effort not to worry me and function during the week, He was taking more and more as his tolerance levels grew. He hadn't told me how bad it was, even when I asked. He thought he was managing them. As did I. I had no idea we had been spiraling downward into a world we never thought possible. He had entered an area no one plans to go: dependency on painkillers.

It didn't start that way. He had jaw surgery, and his doctor had given him the pills. After surgery, a different doctor supported him with his migraines since the surgery didn't fix the problem like it was supposed to. Little did we know it was only creating another one. Tolerance built up for both of us. His tolerance was to the medicine. Mine was having him in pain or escaping pain, leaving me to do all the work. Either way, we were in territory no one wanted to enter, and some had trouble leaving.

DEAD ENDS

Along the way, we can end up on roads we didn't mean to go down. Life, pain, suffering, and choices can cause us to go down paths we think are correct, but in the end, they are not for our good (see Proverbs 14:12). Even when you feel you are paying attention to your heart, what God is doing, or how others' choices affect you, your awareness can become dulled by life. We are human. We must realize we will face pain and we will miss things. Our ability to wade through the delay, trouble, and pain without giving up depends on how we build up our ability to exercise patience. Trying to fix the problem our way will lead to heartache.

Here we sat in heartache. I grieved for the life we had lost. I felt like I had lost connection with my husband. He was always in pain. I didn't get date nights or even help to care for sick kids. Our dog was having seizures, and instead of feeling like part of a team, I felt like I cared for everyone by myself.

I don't know if people knew what I was really going through. Back then, appearances mattered. Having dealt with rejection issues, I was afraid to tell people how I really felt. It is amazing how parts of your life can feel like they are dying, while other parts are full of life. I was busy serving. I was serving my family, my church, and my community. I was doing all the things. In fact, I was doing them well. From the outside, it looked like I had it all together. Some days I did. But there were still parts of my heart and life that were slowly being suffocated, veering further and further down the road towards a dead end.

My husband didn't mean to put us in that situation. He loved God and loved us. But slowly the weight of life, the worries and concerns of providing, and the chronic pain started choking the life out of us. His focus started being drawn to his pain and the disappointment of not seeing healing. Slowly the gaze shifted, and then we gradually veered off course.

Though you might not be experiencing physical pain, we all can find areas where disappointment or wounds have drawn our attention away from truth. Maybe emotional wounds are slowly festering in your heart right now because of something someone has said. Disappointment is easy to get distracted by. Are you frustrated about not getting that promotion? What are the areas in your life you are too busy to address? Remember, not all of my heart was in trouble, only parts of my heart felt like they were slowly dying.

There is good news! When we recognize there are parts of us that need attention or we are on paths we shouldn't be, God is faithful to help us get back on track. He is present with us on every path. Whether we have intentionally turned down the wrong road, made bad decisions, or have some wounded areas, He is not far off. One name for God is Immanuel – God With Us.[3]

I was so relieved to know how close God is when we are in our mess. Even when I found myself in a life I didn't recognize, I knew His healing was just around the corner. Life is hard; it's messy. We have established that, but we may miss how vital one small choice can be. Small choices can lead to a series of other small decisions that slowly lead you to a place you weren't planning on going to. But even so, there is better news. We are never too far from His love!

I didn't see it coming, nor would I have believed you if you had told me we'd be suffering in this way and having to fight through this kind of pain. Loving God and growing up in church doesn't keep you from pain or hardship. Being good teens who go to Bible college and serve as youth leaders, small group leaders, and worship leaders doesn't exclude you from the enemy's tactics. In fact, living in pursuit of God's truth, loving and faithfully serving Him might just put a target on your back. This situation wasn't something we went looking for, but here we were.

I am so grateful God wasn't surprised by where we found ourselves. Instead, His love, compassion, and truth guided us out of the mire. Just like the Bible says, "I waited patiently for the Lord; he turned to me and heard my cry. He lifted me out of the slimy pit, out of the mud and mire, he set my feet on a rock and gave me a firm place to stand" (Psalm 40:1-2 NIV). One day in the middle of our journey, that verse took on a whole new meaning. I had never felt more stuck in the mud than I did walking through the pain of rejection, betrayal, and weariness. But from that place, God's love brought tangible peace, the kind that takes you from a sticky situation and puts you on solid ground.

Those moments, and many more, have given me the opportunity to learn how *wait* and *weight* are both involved in patience. The *wait in patience* involves our gaze fixed on hope. The *weight in patience* requires us to endure circumstances that don't always switch or get fixed quickly. Patience is not easy, and even when we innocently miss the signs, we can turn our attention back to God, looking for his hope, mercy, and grace which helps us endure the hard moments!

When we find ourselves in trouble, in sin, or being directed the wrong way, God is longing for us to call out to Him. That means we turn away from sin and find Him! God knows we can't do this alone, and we can't choose life-giving paths without His help. God sent Jesus. He did more than clear a path; He *became* the path – the bridge between death and life. Maybe you have never heard this before or maybe it didn't make sense to you. It isn't a fantasy story to make life easier. Jesus is life, and choosing Him gives meaning to our life. The choices don't stop when you surrender your life to Jesus. Choosing Him is a daily choice.

Just in case you need to hear this, we need Jesus! From birth, sin has separated us from God's holiness. Even as babies we aren't pure enough to have a relationship with a holy God because of our humanity. So, this is not about veering off course. Whether we think we have gone down the wrong path or not, we can only have a relationship with God because of Jesus. The Bible says that "He is the way, the truth, and the life" (John 14:6 NIV). At every age and stage, we can't live without Him. Children and adults alike get trapped in daily choices and behaviors that lead to death. Jesus lifts us out of the mess and gives us a secure place to stand.

When my husband and I found our marriage, our finances, feelings of rejection and performance, and health choices at a dead end, I am thankful Jesus answered our call. It wasn't easy; we had to fight our way out of it. Our family, friends, and church rallied around us. It required a complete U-turn, and accountability and honesty had to

be our new path. We felt all the feels, things like relief, grief, desperation, and hope. Honestly, there wasn't one magical day when we
turned it all around. As slowly as we wandered down the wrong path,
Jesus led us out. Some of the days after were just as painful, and it
was a constant battle, but Jesus helped us win one small victory at a
time. Dead ends aren't roads you want to journey down, but fighting
to get free and realizing freedom has a name. Jesus is freedom, which
makes all the difference.

DO NOT ENTER

Have you figured it out? When we start leaving behind the familiar,
we will come across obstacles. There is a real enemy who wants to
derail you in our pursuit of God's best for our lives. The Bible says he
is "like a roaring lion seeking whom he may devour" (1 Peter 5:8
NIV). This enemy knows to throw out subtle enticements or to
encourage agreement that we have the right to go where we want
when we want. He wants us to get lost in our suffering, like the
constant daily pain my husband was fighting. The enemy slowly
introduced half-truths which led to medicating himself so he could
function and provide. The chronic and constant pain anesthetized us
to the enemy's ploys because we thought we were dealing with a
natural injury.

The enemy is a liar, let's be clear. He is good at creating distractions and revealing disillusions. He does not want you to have a life of
abundance and of more. Little by little he steals, kills, and destroys
parts of our life. He doesn't just attack our circumstances; he goes for
our identity. His only goal is to bring confusion to what God has said
and who we are – to steer us away from the One who is truth and life.
If we allow it, we get distracted and find ourselves forcing our way
through places we never meant to go. Sometimes we make it through
unscathed, avoiding natural consequences. Other times, we get
marked in the process as we push past barricades which are there for
our good.

Our curiosity or unhappiness with the current road can stir emotions and the desire to fix or change it. There are trails everywhere we can go down to escape from the challenging moments. It's easy to find distraction at the push of a button, sending whatever we want from a virtual shopping cart to our doorstep. We can get lost in reels and streaming movies, and this form of escape has changed our reality.

Culture tells us to pursue happiness above everything else, and if we don't want to do "it," we don't have to. Every generation faces a similar issue. The pioneers set out to provide for themselves and follow the American dream. Some had to fight tirelessly and overcome obstacles to achieve their goal or die trying. Some did it the right way, while others let greed lead them off the safer path. My generation lived between what was and would be. We are a generation who knew how to play outside, longed for efficiency, and fought to make technology serve us. We learned to keep going, no matter what, which left my generation shaking off hurt and not dealing with it. Today's youth are intelligent, aware, and understand many cultures. They have grown up in a world with access to it all. Unfortunately, it has bread entitlement in many, believing they can go wherever they want, whenever they want with no accountability. Knowing which generation you are part of, and what mindsets you cling to is important. Whatever category you relate to, we can't make our own way.

As a child, I lived in the Pacific Northwest and loved it! Everywhere we went, we found adventure. We played for hours in the woods behind our house, where we built the tree house every kid dreams about. When we weren't playing there, we would go on nature walks to pick berries or visit our friends who owned an incredible piece of land. They had barns, horses, and hay bales that we used to create forts. Adventure was all around us. We didn't need to leave the safety of their yard to have fun, but there was an entire property to explore. Outside the immediate area were trees, streams, fields, and mystery that piqued our curiosity and awaited our discovery.

I remember cutting through fields, ducking under fences, and spending hours exploring. One day, we ignored the wire in front of us. No gate was nearby, so I fit my body between the two wires, squeezing through the opening. I had almost made it entirely through when the buzz hit my ear first and then my whole body. It stung and rattled me to the core. The fence was electrified! I had missed the sign that told me this was a dangerous path, so I wasn't expecting it. It was a horrible feeling, and I will never forget it. In tears, with my ear bleeding, I went back to the house. That journey ended. The lesson I learned was that shortcuts can hurt.

So many of us find ourselves in this type of situation. We want to see the world, find happiness, and explore all our options. We think our life is an internet shopping cart, and we try on churches. We scroll through friendships or try on relationships, knowing we can *return* them with one click and get a refund. Unfortunately, it doesn't always cross our minds that we can't slide our way through a fence to get to the other side. Taking the set path can help keep us safe instead of the fence-hopping shortcut to happiness. The grass is not always greener, and shortcuts can hurt!

God has designed us to desire goodness, to pursue joy, and want fulfillment. But often, our options or priorities distract us or convince us that what we have is insufficient. That's why God's Word warns us to, "Set your gaze on the path before you. With fixed purpose, looking straight ahead, ignoring life's distractions. Watch where you're going! Stick to the path of truth, and the road will be safe and smooth before you" (Prov 4:25-26 TPT). When the road gets rocky, we should be searching for life, not running from it.

I don't know about you, but I want to have confidence I am on a good path. Living each day trying to create my own way won't work. The Bible says there is success when we let the Lord determine our steps. He will lead us in the right way, a life-giving way that avoids unnecessary hazards. The slit in my ear healed, but the memory of that sting reminds me that it's safest to take a path meant for us and our good.

Wrong ways are painful. The tears I shed as a girl didn't compare to the many shed during the months of watching my husband get free from painkillers. However, both were impactful. Don't ignore the signs that tell us an area is off-limits or there is a dead-end ahead; we should pay attention! God wants to lead us on smooth paths. He goes before us, leading us down paths He has already cleared. His steps stomp out the rough places. As we follow Him, we can walk on a smooth way.

God doesn't stop us from pursuing adventure; He wants to go with us on the journey. As we go, He desires that we tune our ears to His voice and follow His lead down good paths toward our destination. God is patient with us. He knows we will be tempted to walk away, follow our own thoughts, and fall in the mud. His patience is with us every step of the way, just waiting for us to turn our gaze back to His righteousness. He longs to make our steps firm. Even if we stumble, God will hold our hand and lead us through (see Psalm 37:23).

What moments in your life came about because you chose to break through the wrong way, turning down a dead-end road or crossing a barricade you should never have? Did you make an agreement with friends that led you down destructive paths? Are you entertaining a thought life that keeps you from staying pure or true to your spouse? Maybe you are tempted to jump the fence of your job or church because the grass is more tempting on the other side. It is not wrong to desire love, fulfillment, and happiness. God designed us to want and pursue abundance. However, going after things that are not meant for us is not going after more.

No matter how big or small we have blown it (and we will blow it), the enemy can't rob us of our destiny if we don't hand it to him. We can take it back! Mistakes don't define us; we are defined by our identity in Christ. What He has already done for us on the cross has given us back the legal right to true happiness, which is better defined as joy and abundance.

I want to encourage you; God has given us this life to live well.

He wants us to find joy, be fulfilled, and live with purpose. We are built for longevity. God designed you for eternity; you are destined for more. Going after more is about walking in true identity. He promises that He has good plans for us. Our future is full of hope, and if you look wholeheartedly, you will find Him and see the path He has set before you: toward destiny!

The enemy can't rob us of our destiny if we don't hand it to him.

Questions and Reflections
...to ponder on your way to possibilities!

~

➤What area of disappointment or discouragement is plaguing you?

➤What is your biggest distraction, or what are the areas in your life that seem too big to address?

➤How do you feel after reading the following? "I waited patiently for the Lord; he turned to me and heard my cry. He lifted me out of the slimy pit, out of the mud and mire, he set my feet on a rock and gave me a firm place to stand" (Psalm 40:1-2 NIV).

➤What half truth or complete lie are you believing about your situation?

➤What does God want you to take away from the following verse? "Set your gaze on the path before you. With fixed purpose, looking straight ahead, ignoring life's distractions. Watch where you're going! Stick to the path of truth, and the road will be safe and smooth before you" (Proverbs 4:25-26 TPT).

6

FOLLOW THE SIGNS

THERE MAY HAVE BEEN fingernail marks on the dashboard, but we saw the sign. Thankfully, we escaped stopping in the middle of the intersection. That is when I took a deep breath and thanked God for the signs...and seatbelts! Signs prepare us for what comes ahead and protect us from what could be.

Teaching teenagers to drive has given me a massive appreciation for signs. Yes, I have now lived through three teens learning to drive. Each experience has been different, and I have relaxed a little more with each one. I was a little more nervous with the first, not because he was a horrible driver, but because I had never given up so much control. Putting your life in inexperienced hands can cause some anxiety. That said, I was constantly thankful for the speed limit signs reaffirming my advice to slow down!

WHICH WAY

Most of the time, we are looking around and aware of signs coming up. However, detour signs usually come out of nowhere. These temporary signs in regular traffic can take us by surprise. Sometimes, detours seem like a nuisance. They often take us in a less direct and less convenient way. However, if we view it with the right mindset, we can see the value and benefit of taking new directions. Detours can get us to step outside of our comfort zones – the bubbles we get used to living in. After all, that bubble can pop in a matter of seconds, and the only thing you can do is find a new way.

Detours get our minds working actively. They force us to no longer cruise on autopilot. Instead, we are required to pay attention and look around for signs to be sure we go the right way. Then, you finally spot it again, and your heart beats, not lulled to sleep by the common. Sounds become crisp, and sights become vibrant as you go a new way. The route, the direction, and even the manner of travel feels fresh. I get it, change is hard for some, and that might have you associating a detour with a negative, uncomfortable, and inconvenient hassle. Annoyed we are not on the right or most efficient path, we feel uncomfortable.

Though our final destination is important, I hope you understand this life is about so much more! Our destiny is not summed up by the end destination. The destination is where we land. Living is where we walk, travel, and how we choose to navigate the streets with all of their stops, starts, and even detours. Detours don't have to derail us from our destiny. We can find the most scenic and fascinating routes while taking a detour.

When referring to detours, I am not just talking about the detours we experience in the natural realm on earth. It is also important to note that detours are not the hardships in this life. Detours take us around those places and move us out of harm's way. They can get us beyond the frustrations of life. Sometimes a friend's encouraging words can detour you out of self-pity. Sometimes a song can detour you out of despair. A smile, a hug, or even an understanding nod detours us from sorrow, bringing us to a new path of joy. Detours take us to new places, so rest assured, detours are helpful and don't derail us from destiny. On the contrary, they direct us toward it!

Spiritually speaking, my destination is heaven. More than that, my destination is not my destiny. Our destiny is comprised of *successive nows*! Every moment of now creates and forms our identity, which becomes destiny if we partner with it. My destiny is to learn how to love and be loved by a merciful and faithful God. It is also to discover my gifts and how I can add value to those around me; when I do, I live with purpose. Specifically, my destiny is learning how to be who God has designed me to be. Remember, destiny is not just found in the destination. My destination includes landing next to a God who is my Savior, life, love, and ultimate source. He is my destiny. He is my safe harbor.

TRANSITION

I love to walk along the coastline on a sunny afternoon, just as the sun is going to set. The reflective light glistens on each wave's ripples, and my heart relaxes at the view. I breathe in deeply, exhale, and tension exits my body. Those moments are magical. As I walk between the wet and dry sand, I listen to the gentle rhythm of the constant waves rolling in. In the distance, sailboats glide through the water, propelled by the gentle breeze which can be felt on my face.

Today was one of those beautiful days, and I enjoyed watching the boats as they made their way to and from the harbor. Finally, I arrived at the jetty and climbed onto the massive stone structure. Carefully stacked boulders of all sizes created a solid structure. I walked along the flat surface created by concrete that had been added to solidify the jetty.

The view from the jetty was beautiful. You could see sailboats on the open water and those docked in the harbor. I loved all the different colored sails and neatly rolled cords. The port was at peace. The boats had made it safely into the harbor, and were there to rest, refuel, and get renewed focus for their next trip.

The harbor was secured on every side by a strong wall of boulders, tightly constructed and cemented, providing a barrier between the vast ocean and the sheltered harbor. As a result, the rough waters could not access the inlet leading into the harbor. This rock barrier created a place for the rough waters to hit and be redirected, lessening the constant barrage of the tide. There on the inlet's pathway to the harbor, the boats could transition. The sails used in the open water were now lowered for the boat's return to the dock.

Similar to the boat, there are seasons when we are happy and content in the open waters of our assignments. Fulfilling what we are created to do and pursuing adventure is what brings joy. Then, at the end of those periods when our roles or assignments have changed, it's necessary to make our way back to port before going out on the next adventure.

Choosing to rest and refuel looks different than being forced to dock because of destruction or lack. A boat may enter the harbor looking for safety or rest because it has had a hard sail, but the opposite is also true. Those who have had a fun day at sea, enjoying their adventure, also come to dock. Rest is not just for the weary, it is also for those who enjoyed the ride but need to refuel and renew vision in between trips. It is a time to readjust, replenish supplies, and connect with communities on dry land.

Like this sailboat, we were not made to be in motion all of the time. We were created to be led by the wind of the Spirit out on assignment, but also use the power of the Word to bring us back to a place of rest. This step is vital for our journey. With us being the captains of our own boat, He is with us to lead us through the torrents and also lead us back into the safety of still waters to refocus and reposition. I love how the Passion Translation calls Jesus my, "best friend and my shepherd." He not only knows what we need, but He provides for us, giving us, "more than enough. He offers a resting place for me in His luxurious love . . . in an oasis of peace near *the quiet brook of bliss*. That's where he restores and revives my life" (Psalm 23:1-3 TPT). He leads us into safety and into a peaceful rest. He is our safe harbor.

There is an incredible word we don't use often in our everyday speech: *repose*. It is a noun that Merriam-Webster's Dictionary describes as, "the state of resting after exertion...a place of rest, peace or tranquility...the lack of activity or movement."[4] It's also a verb that can mean *situated or kept in a particular place*. This resting harbor is key to our journey. We must have moments of intentionally being reposed, brought into harbor after a season or leg of our journey has ended.

Repose is not just about rest; it is the act of positioning or sometimes re-positioning. Detours can remind us that in order to get to new places and spaces, sometimes we must first find rest and reposition first.

This book is the direct result of a life detour that transitioned me into a new space. Just weeks before writing, my function and roles in ministry looked different. I was serving my local church community in a new way during the height of the pandemic. It felt like the pandemic thrust me into the role, but I know it was God. He brought it my way to challenge me, invoke growth, and use me in a greater way. It was a busy season of finding a new rhythm amidst so much change. All of us on the team had lives, families, jobs, and responsibilities outside of ministry. We all faced struggles while navigating uncharted waters of political chaos, health issues, fear, and all the in-between.

That season was an adventure. It was like being in a sailboat out in open waters. There were incredible times of catching the wind and gliding over the expanse. There were definitely sun-in-our-face, birds-flying-overhead moments. We also faced nail biting, clinging onto hope while challenging storms raged around us. Sometimes it's best to hold on tight and press straight into the torrents; other times, situations require you to turn yourself around, catch the wind that moves you away from a path, and go in a new direction.

There came a moment in my journey when it was time to reassess if God wanted me to continue in this role. My heart desires to do what God asks me to do or be where He asks me to be. I never want to move or steer my life without His guidance. I have done that before, and it doesn't work! In the middle of praying about the current season and asking for clarity about the next season, detour signs were visible.

COMMUNICATION

As I mentioned, God loves to use language that makes sense to us. He is a good Father and knows how to talk to each of His children individually. Each child will hear things differently, and a good parent does their best to communicate in a way to help them understand. For me, God often uses concepts in nature to show me principles, but just as often, He uses numbers! I love how God created our minds and set things in motion using time and math to make them relatable for us humans. There is order in God's creativity, and as you look through the stories of the Bible, you will often see numbers repeated or used to symbolize specific things.

Quick side note: though numbers can have a meaning, God doesn't always communicate using just one meaning. God is said to be three in one: Father, Son, and Holy Spirit. In Scripture, you will see Jesus was in the tomb three days before rising from the dead. Foreshadowing this, Jonah sat in the belly of a whale for three days! God used this number to represent God, rebirth, and salvation. This doesn't mean the number three *only* means these things when they appear to us. It might have a personal significance to you as the third child or as an important date to you. Through your filter, it might have a different personal meaning. This is why having an intimate relationship with God, knowing *who* He is and *how* He communicates with us, is vital as we journey through life!

For me, repeated numbers get my attention. I can go for months, through entire seasons, where I don't ever see a repeated number on a clock. Then, one day it shifts. Without looking for them, I start to see them *everywhere and all the time.* When this happens, I make notes in my journal, or now with technology I can take screenshots on my phone. During this most recent season, I constantly came across 1:11 or 11:11 on the microwave clock or my phone. In the past, that language pointed me toward two things: oneness and transition. I understood to keep my heart and ear attentive to the Father, remaining in oneness with Him while navigating the transition.

I paid attention and continually asked the Father if this was a time of transition or if these little signs were pointing toward something else. I sensed the shift coming. From one moment to the next, I went from knowing exactly what my schedule and role consisted of to having an empty plate. The sudden re-positioning of goals and purpose felt abrupt. My heart, mind, and emotions were all over the place. I felt both excitement for a new season and deep sadness that the roles and purpose I had been journeying through were over. There was a sense of freedom, relief, sorrow, grief, and even panic in the *not knowing*. Though every emotion was present, my heart had a stabilizer. I knew God was inviting me into oneness as we walked through this transition together.

Looking back at the week before the sudden shift, I realize that if my life was that sailboat, the sail had been lowered and the Word of God was propelling me towards the shore. My view changed from being in open waters to the entrance into the harbor. There were jetties on both sides, the walls had gone up, and I was now separated from what had been. I was separated from any identity or assignment I had in that season or role. The waters of my heart, which had been in panic and turbulence from the shift, began to calm. My Good Captain led me into the harbor, towards the dock, where I would get a chance to rest, refuel, and replenish before my next adventure.

Some of these pages were birthed from the moments of stillness I had in the harbor, in the transition. Truly, the detour I was experiencing was for my good and the good of what God had for me next. The detour signs prepared my heart for the transition. One important lesson I have learned is that detours don't derail, they direct. My destiny and purpose on the earth have not changed. It is to know who He is and who I am. My pursuit of His heart and voice so I can live from a place of value has not changed. The repositioning just changes where my energy is directed.

Signs signal essential information. Detours can be for our good; they get us around an area of construction that is not for us to go through, or they get us back on track after climbing the fence. Paying attention to how God communicates with us is crucial to our success. It is vital for our growth, identity, and ultimately our path of purpose. We have seen how red-light moments give us time to ask questions, and detours give us a time of transition to reassess and re-ask about assignments.

PATIENCE'S WORK

Patience is a lesson we must embrace as we go after the impossible things God has planned for us. Patience is necessary as we learn about questions, listen, and stay alert to what is happening around us. Patience involves bearing the suffering and believing even when we haven't seen the answer come. For instance, we had to bear the weight of my husband's chronic pain and our infertility. It caused us to develop and grow due to the patience necessary to wait, believe, and navigate hard things. Many struggle to find jobs and overcome diagnosis and disease. I stand with close family and friends, waiting for their breakthroughs to come in these areas. Patience is not one of those lessons we learn once. It is constant work because some questions may not be answered until we get to heaven. For instance, why did those bad things happen? Why did we face financial struggles? Why did that loved one get sick, suffer, or die?

God is not afraid of our questions. Questions are good and serve to teach us, give us experience, and allow us to hear different viewpoints. Asking them signifies life; it means you are awake, aware, observant, and curious! But there is more. Listening for the answer or lesson is what allows us to grow and advance. This dialogue between asking and seeking is what I consider the forward momentum of our journey. It is what keeps us from remaining stationary. Even if it propels us forward just a little, there is still movement.

Patience is needed. But when we see how it relates to a heart that wants more, patience becomes crucial. It is one of the components we must develop, choose, and implement. When we embrace it, it helps us face all the moments that don't make sense – all the challenging moments that don't seem fair. Patience requires us to endure weightiness. We must learn to follow God's voice and heart, especially through the obstacles of life.

Whether we are actively waiting for a breakthrough or going after our next assignment, we risk the comfortable and familiar. Reflecting on the last few chapters, we see how vital patience is. Looking ahead, we will discuss how choices matter. We can numb the pain and frustration, or we can set our gaze on a higher perspective. Ultimately, taking a deeper look into the *why* of our journey enables us to become more aware of our attitudes and position – whether seated, standing, walking, running, or climbing!

Destiny is comprised of successive nows.

Questions and Reflections
...to ponder on your way to possibilities!

❧

➤What is one way God has saved you from a harmful thing? What positive detour have you experienced?

➤If "patience involves bearing the suffering and believing even when we haven't seen the answer come," then what area of your life is patience at work in you?

➤What do you think the following statement means? "Our destiny is comprised of *successive nows!*"

➤When have you experienced times of repose? Knowing that "repose is not just about rest; it is the act of positioning or sometimes re-positioning," in what ways did those moments impact your journey?

➤What are some of the ways you sense God speaking to you, i.e., numbers, dreams, songs, pictures, nature, etc.?

Part two

ATTITUDE

7

ALTITUDE MATTERS

ATTITUDE IS key in any journey and can be defined as the way we approach a situation, how we think, how we respond, how we react, or how we advance. What kind of attitude we have can be the thing that advances us *up into understanding or down into defeat*. Attitude is everything. Whether our circumstances are good or bad, our heart, mind, and response will determine success or failure. Success is a funny thing...defining it can be subjective. Better yet, *who* defines it? What does it look like? During this journey of discovering destiny and purpose, we can limit our own success. Sadly, we may forget that the process is just as important as the product.

Attitude is only as good as the perspective and belief system it comes from. Our outward behavior stems from internal churnings; we act according to what we think, see, and feel. If we are internally struggling with fear, anger, bitterness, or loss, our external behavior exhibits those core beliefs. If I am afraid, I might try to control the world around me. If I am bitter, my actions might be mean or distrustful.

Beliefs and perspectives dictate our attitudes, which then bleed out into our actions. Using the proverbial half-empty glass can help us understand this. If we see the glass as only half full, we are working from a negative perspective that only views the limitations and lack. We notice what we don't have or what is missing. This leaves us wanting more and never content or joyful with what we do have. Our actions show we are never satisfied, becoming angry if we don't have what we want.

Using the same analogy, if our perspective clings onto the positive aspects of our situations and struggles, we function from the belief that we have something. Though small or large, we are not without. There is space in the other half, giving us room for more! This perspective breeds actions that are hopeful and expectant. This perspective lives in forward movement instead of getting stuck with what is not. The negative heart gets stopped in its tracks, but the heart content and yet ready for more makes room to go into places only dreamed of.

I am learning that proper perspective sets us on a course to journey through life well. Perspective sets our mind and heart in a place of protection from the darkness around us. When we guard our thinking, our beliefs (internal perspective) remain healthy. Healthy beliefs then set us up for actions that are not dictated by our environment. Healthy perspectives facilitate victory and give us the chance to *change* our environment, not be a victim of it. A positive perspective allows us to see life in the most unlikely of places. Our attitudes and choices give us the opportunity to climb to new heights.

NEW HEIGHTS

One day, I saw things shift with my physical eyes. Leaving early that morning, I was ready to make the long trek up the mountain to pick our kids up from their youth summer camp. Pulling out of the driveway felt like any other day. I had music, coffee, and expectation to see my kids and hear all the stories about their incredible week. As

I drove away from my neighborhood, I reached for my coffee and suddenly drove straight into a thick patch of fog. It was dense and surrounded me on every side. I could barely see the car in front of me, and instantly was full of dread. Would the next two hours be this slow, tense, and dark?

At the base of the mountain, the fog was just as thick. I felt as if I was up against a curtain of gray. I couldn't see far in front of me, and I couldn't see the sky above. It was dark, and again I noticed anxiety stirring in my heart. I imagine most people dread driving in these conditions and do not enjoy being slapped in the face with a wall of fog. I admit, there was apprehension bordering on panic at the thought of driving the winding roads up the mountain surrounded by this thick haze that impaired my vision.

My hands tightened on the steering wheel, but I began slowly making progress up the mountain. With my eyes focused on the nose of my car and the sliver of road that I could see, I moved forward. With every curve up, I saw a little more of the road in front of me. Slowly, the fog began to thin. My hands loosened, the white knuckles faded, and my rigid back began to relax. With the increase in altitude, portions of the sky began to peek through, and light seeped through the clouds. The sky grew brighter, and my heart returned to a steady rhythm.

Ascending the mountain, the winding climb to a higher elevation led me away from the gray and into a more transparent sky. I was relieved. Though the journey was nerve-wracking, I was being led out of the darkness into a more spacious place. Then, after one turn, I was surrounded by brilliant light. The sun was full, bright, and beaming out above a thick carpet of white. Stunned, I had to pull over at the turnout to look over the valley below. The sight was incredible. High above the clouds was sunshine and blue sky, while below my feet was nothing but a thick ocean of dense white clouds. From that higher place, the view was spectacular. The climb had changed everything.

Above the horizon displayed a polar opposite view to the one below. When I had been driving below surrounded by the thick fog, it was intense – a great nuisance and distraction. Stuck beneath this sea of white, it had been dark and dreary, stirring up anxious feelings. Yet from these heights, the sun shone down on a blanket of white, which reflected the joyful and hope-filled light of the sun. From this viewpoint, the clouds sang of splendor, though from underneath the same clouds had felt like darkness.

WE MUST RISE

Altitude Matters! As I went higher, I rose above the circumstances below. Standing above it all, my soul filled with sunlight, freedom, peace, and joy. It was as if I had followed a spiral highway to the top, bringing me to openness and clarity. Listen to how this version states it, "Lovers of God walk on a highway of light and their way shines brighter" (Proverbs 4:8 TPT). Looking out from the mountain over the valley below, I had confidence that I could carry hope down into the distractions and anxiety of the fog-filled valley. Altitude had not changed the situations I woke up to; my circumstances had not changed. I had the same bills, the same health, the same family, the same job, and car. Life had not changed as I moved up in elevation, only my perspective had. (We will look at this more in the next chapter.)

In a matter of moments, the view had changed my outlook which had in turn changed the atmosphere of my heart. My new altitude offered me a new perspective which changed my attitude. Altitude and access became so intertwined in my understanding. I had a fresh vantage point and fresh vitality. At that moment, above the clouds, I was reminded that God had given me access to both sides of the horizon. God gave me a gift that day. As I went back to real life, struggles, joys, and sorrows, I realized I had a choice and ability to pull from the hope, joy, and freedom I found when I was up above the thickness.

Access is an interesting thing. It means a couple of different things. First, we see that without it, we can't get into certain areas. It is the very meaning of unlocking places and spaces we want to enter. Second, access means I can attain what is in those places. For me, altitude is what creates permission in our hearts and mind to access the thoughts of God. His wisdom and His ability to see the broader picture can only be seen from a vantage point high above the daily struggles. In fact, there is a verse in Proverbs that articulates this idea perfectly. The promise states, "For the Lord has a hidden storehouse of wisdom made accessible to his godly lovers" (Prov 2:7 PROMISE).

Plain and simple, perspective gives us access to God's wisdom and into God's heart. He makes these mysteries and truths available to those who love Him and who seek to rise above the distractions, for even a glimpse of truth. Lifting our eyes opens the door of our understanding and the space of our hearts to connect with the wisdom of God.

This rising and attaining are what we need for this journey. This access gives an opportunity along the way to leave behind the everyday messes and the everyday stresses, for that moment of greater understanding and renewed hope. I am convinced that if we could visit this high place more often (or even live from that higher place), then our journey would exceed our wildest hopes and dreams. New hope, God's hope, would be attained as our physical and spiritual eyes moved off our problems and above the distractions of everyday life. Instead, our attention would be put squarely on the One who sees it all. Altitude and access to God's heart and mind are the key to pursuing the more we long for. Even when other people's opinions surround us or our own desires surface, our hearts will only find joy and fulfillment as we stay fixed on the only opinion or truth that matters: God's.

Part of realizing how altitude impacts the way we walk is seeing, from God's heart and perspective, which areas of our life need to be addressed. From the high places, we are able to see areas of our lives that need healing. Some of my journey has involved stepping back into the fog to visit areas of my life where I experienced trauma, pain, or judgment.

If we want to progress, we must assess those internal wounded places to ensure that the hope we experience on the mountaintop brings restoration and freedom to the valley below. This is how altitude and access are born from patience. Ascending to get wisdom requires patience during the climb. It is not an overnight trip, and we cannot effectively travel on the ground without first climbing above the fog to gain fresh hope. The mountain-top view allows us to gather hope and find new energy to return to the darker places and do the work. Sleeves rolled up with new determination, we can bring light into any areas of our heart or mind that need healing.

CLING TO HOPE

Remember when we talked about Abraham's obedience to leave behind the familiar in pursuit of more? That risk was rooted in his faith. Sometimes people think faith includes following blindly. We will look at faith more later, but let me just say Abraham had internal eyes that could see God's nature and faithfulness. Because of this, Abraham was able to cling to hope and journey towards destiny. He trusted God. That faith and hope gave him confidence in the waiting and directed him toward impossibilities.

Like Abraham, our life can become a picture of natural versus supernatural as we fight past man's perspective and hold tight to the promises of what God said would be. It was a constant internal fight to press toward the land promised to him. Abraham became a father, despite his aging body, because he "considered him faithful who had made the promise" (Hebrews 11:11 NIV). Faith puts value in things hoped for; faith says God's promises and reality consist of more than what our natural senses tell us. Faith walks and lives with this perspective of promise. What God says should dictate our actions, above feeling and sight. Like Abraham, we can cling to hope, or better yet, "wrap your heart tightly around the hope that lives within us, knowing that God always keeps his promises" (Hebrews 10:23 TPT).

It is always a good idea to go back to the original language and see the word that was used, along with the original context and meaning. The writer of Hebrews used the Greek word *katecho*[5] for the word hold, cling, or wrap your heart tightly around. By definition, it communicates that we can maintain possession by holding firmly or being wrapped up (fastened) to hope. There is human responsibility involved in gripping something. It is not a passive task. We do it with intention and strength. Fastening ourselves to hope is much like harnessing ourselves to a parasail. We lock ourselves into the harness which attaches us to the sail with ropes. When connected, we are anchored to the boat, and yet able to soar high above it all. Have you ever been parasailing? I have...

The moment I was first whisked up into the air, I let out a scream that could have broken glass. Excited and afraid, I inched higher and higher as the boat and waving passengers became smaller. I couldn't believe the feeling of being that high over such depths. I was thankful for and dependent on that harness. It gave me freedom to be lifted hundreds of feet above it all and still feel safe! Hope fastens us to God's promises which are for our good. Knowing that we can be fastened to His truth (high above our situations) allows us to have security, even in moments when our feet are far from the ground and we have no control. Staying connected in hope to His plan for our lives lifts us over the ground-level problems.

So, let's look at our lives and contemplate what we are fastened to. Are you holding onto your own willpower? Are you clinging to what others say about you? Is your hope in your job or savings account? What things are you fastened to? There is a point where we must figure out where our expectations are focused and who or what motivates our anticipation for the future.

Expectation and anticipation are at the root of the Greek word for the hope[6] (katecho) we wrap ourselves around. Hope is described as confidence that God is who He says He is and does what He says

He will do. We don't cling to something that will hurt us or destroy us. No, we cling to what is good, and if that good thing lives in us, we fasten ourselves to Him! Like a parasail, hope lifts us higher. Altitude matters!

Attitude is what creates permission in our hearts and mind to access the thoughts of God.

Questions and Reflections
...to ponder on your way to possibilities!

➤What do you think the following statement means? "Perspective sets our mind and heart in a place of protection from the darkness around us."

➤What does this verse mean to you? "Lovers of God walk on a highway of light and their way shines brighter" (Proverbs 4:8 TPT).

➤If, "Perspective gives us access to God's wisdom and into God's heart," then what ways are you shifting your attitude, altitude, or perspective?

➤Knowing that "if we want to progress, we must assess those internal wounded places to ensure that the hope we experience on the mountaintop brings restoration and freedom to the valley below," what wounds have you identified? How are you addressing the internal wounds?

➤What does the following verse change for you or mean to you? "Wrap your heart tightly around the hope that lives within us, knowing that God always keeps his promises" (Hebrews 10:23 TPT).

8

ASCENDING HIGHER

THE HOUSE WAS EMPTY. Every possession we owned had been sold or boxed up and moved out. I sat on the floor of what I thought would be my forever home and wept. I grieved the dreams we had carried for that space and the plans we had made. My heart ached for the loss and the uncertainty of what was ahead. The only thought in my mind was, *how will we get past this?* The sick feeling in my stomach wouldn't go away. So, I sat, wept, and prayed.

We had moved out, and although the house remained empty, it had not been sold yet. Feeling like there was no other option, we put the house on the market. My mind reeled with repetitive thoughts like, *how did we get here?* The only answer now was to short sale our home and get out from the upside-down mortgage that weighed heavy on us. Like many others in that season, the recession hit us, and our ARM-mortgage jumped from manageable to double what we had planned for. This wasn't how we saw things going...at all. Though we prayed for a different kind of miracle, the house now displayed a *for sale* sign on our lawn.

Even with a promise, it's not always easy to know what your breakthrough or miracle could look like. We have discussed how

Abraham had a hard time figuring out how his heir would come, and how Ezekiel was waiting to see how God would fulfill what he saw in his vision. Both had promises from God and were required to lean into intimacy to see breakthroughs come. We won't have it all figured out, but those who went before us give us insight into ways God can do it for us!

King David is another who walked through obstacles in pursuit of more. Before becoming king, he was infamously known as the boy with a rock who took down a giant named Goliath. He was a worshiper and shepherd, which means he understood about high places. He traveled them with his sheep, learning how to climb and fight like a warrior, ascending higher.

PERSPECTIVE

David understood that perspective was attained in the high places. He knew it wasn't about a physical high place, but understood the importance of changing his gaze to find truth about his situation from what God spoke. Time spent with God taught David that promises accompanied perspective. By leaving behind mindsets fixed on earthly problems, concerns, and anxieties, David was able to position his thoughts higher. From that place he was able to see God's promises for life, abundance, and salvation. David stayed present in the moments requiring patience. In between bears, battles, and bullies, David found quiet time to get alone with God and pull heaven's mindset down. His heart's cry was to know God and praise His name.

David reminds us of the importance of going after truth instead of the narrow thinking we gather from what our earthly eyes see. In wisdom, he reminds us to, "Fix your heart on the promises of God, and you will dwell in the land, feasting on his faithfulness" (Psalm 37:3-4 TPT). What an incredibly powerful thought. Our heart can cling to what God has promised, even when our eyes don't see it from below. Harnessing, fixing, and clinging to God's faithfulness, allows us to access the high places so we can better occupy the land.

There's no need to rush to the next thing. Instead, we are encouraged to find delight in God alone; intimacy in the high places gives us what is needed to transform our attitudes and thinking. Trusting in His timing, direction, and wisdom changes our mindset, giving us an advantage in this life. The right attitude gives us the positioning required to go after our purpose. It provides space for the deeper planting of promise that is coming. David understood about creating a place for growth and expansion.

David learned the importance of finding delight in the Lord. He knew his God would come to his aid and lead him ahead in the way he should go. These very same moments are available to us, allowing us to slow us down and calm our heart. I am convinced that our ability to *rise above* circumstances and above emotion is a key component to successfully going after all God has for us. Ascending higher provides perspective and clarity to refocus on the big picture. David wrote, "Those who trust in the LORD will inherit the land . . . the humble of heart will inherit every promise and enjoy abundant peace" (Psalm 37:9,11 TPT).

EMPTY SPACE

Fighting to hold onto peace, I sat in our empty house waiting to see how God would fulfill His promises because I knew he would. He always had. Today would be no different. In a season of uncertainty, our church family (which met at a public high school on Sundays) needed a place to host a prayer meeting. I felt that tug in my heart to use the empty house. It was a risk, but I told the real estate agent to note no showings that day. We were giving up prime showing time on that Saturday, but I felt the nudge to create space for prayer and fasting. Our hearts longed to see God show up for so many of our church family who needed various kinds of miracles.

To backtrack, this house has a rich legacy of worship and prayer.

This house had hosted worship gatherings, Bible studies, and countless prayer meetings. Sown into every wall and floorboard was a legacy of faith that God could do the impossible. It started long before we moved in. Family friends had owned that home before us, and we spent hours there as teens and even sat in those rooms as adults praying for the children who were promised to us. We had encountered God's direction in times of uncertainty and experienced an outpouring of the Holy Spirit in the back room as we prayed through some of our family's darkest moments.

Now, our church family showed up to this empty house to walk the open hallways and pray. Personal and corporate times of prayer and praise lingered in the atmosphere. We spent the day believing for miracles. The moments were precious.

Although agents were not supposed to show the house, we had a few interruptions. People assumed that since the house was vacant, it didn't matter when they showed up. When buyers came, people politely asked the agent to show the house later. Later in the day, another person came to the door. Like others before them, they were turned away by one of our friends. However, as they were being turned away, something in me said, "*Stop!*" I had that familiar tug in my heart and began running after them to permit them to enter. I explained what we were doing, and they agreed to quietly go through the space.

Our prayer that day was for breakthrough. We prayed for many with disease, financial hardship, addictions, and relationship struggles. In that empty house, we believed for dreams to be fulfilled and miracles to be seen. Not knowing when or how God would answer, we simply showed up and created space to believe, pray, and watch.

Weeks after that prayer meeting, we signed documents selling our house. That day, we found out the name of the new owners; it just happened to be buyers who came to our prayer meeting that day. They were given permission to walk the grounds and given access into that sacred space. It was not easy to hand over the keys to what had been God's provision for our family. We had spent hours of blood, sweat, and tears creating a place we wanted to stay forever. Yet, we knew the provision was not tied to that home. Instead, the new owners, whose last name is pronounced "pray," received a home with a legacy of faith, prayer, and worship. It was all because we followed the nudge of the Holy Spirit and made space for a miracle.

That wasn't the result I was initially contending for. However, as I look back, I see God's faithfulness in it all. Even when things didn't change in the way I wanted them to, He directed my steps. Even when we don't understand the breakthrough, His voice directs. If we choose to listen and obey, we can see Him show up.

I have learned perseverance and obedience are like a well-worn path that opens our hearts and situations to receive the miracle. That path and the open space of humility connect our heart to God's ability. In our personal situations, our determination, trust, and obedience allowed us to see provisions attached to the promises. Even when it looks uncertain, I am confident God's promises and provision will bring peace.

Rising above the reality we live in means viewing the external and internal "temperature" of our soul from a vantage point higher than man's philosophies and understanding. This means putting challenges, opinions, judgments, hurt, grief, and fleshly desires under our feet. Choosing to stand and being determined to walk according to the truths God speaks requires us to know His Word and voice better than the world's voice. Knowing His mindset, His view, and the power of His promise allows us to keep our feet on the ground while having our minds in the heavens.

We no longer have to view our steps as one or the other – positive or negative. There will be mountaintop encounters and valley experiences. That's life. Thankfully, we can also walk through everyday moments full of resources and hope from heaven. We can learn to live from both realities. We can fully understand this world's circumstances while accessing heaven's realities in our situations and relationships. From a mindset high above natural thinking, we can access the resources of heaven with no limitations.

PROMISES

Two significant things are necessary to live from higher thinking. They are so intertwined you almost can't separate them, and together they provide space for heaven to touch earth. Elevated thinking comes from knowing that God has given us a seat to reign with Him. Ephesians explains that "we are seated with Christ in heavenly places" because God has "made known to us the mysteries" so together with Christ, we can "bring all things in heaven and on earth together. (Ephesians 2:6; 1:10 NIV). With faith and expectation, we can declare, "May your kingdom come soon. May your will be done on earth, as it is in heaven" (Matthew 6:10 TPT).

There is a woman in history who, because of faith and expectation, opened up the heavens. Because she had confidence in what she knew to be true (perspective), even though it was not yet fully seen (promise), she created space for a miracle. From the first mention of her name, we recognize she did not shrink back when faced with impossibility. Young and ready for marriage, she has the most famous pregnancy and birth story ever recorded. It can't get more impossible than a virgin being told she would give birth to God's Son. Walking through disbelief and ridicule, Mary had to figure out how to process a promise that sounded unrealistic. How does one get through that and decide to carry, cherish, and steward a promise that would take the impossible and make it possible? Somehow Mary knew that nothing is truly impossible when God is involved, and she declared, "May it be to me as you have said" (Luke 1:38 NIV).

Fast forward, her promised child became a man. She knew He was destined for great things, and it was only a matter of time before everyone saw the truth. Though sent for more, He first lived a regular life as a carpenter, shopped at the market, played with the village kids, and went to celebrations. Then, one day it all changed.

The party had begun. Friends and family ate, celebrated, and drank the abundance of wine. After many hours of celebration, the supply of wine came to an end. As a mom, I can imagine Mary hearing that the wine had been used up and springing into action to find a solution. Knowing the panic and what is involved in taking care of guests is something I share with Mary. In fact, the last celebration I put on for my twin girls was a special one. I spent many hours collecting the right dishes, buying the right food, and stocking up on Sparkling Cider so their picnic in Historic Balboa Park could be perfect! As the sun was setting, they danced by the coy pond as a classical guitarist played. Glittered champagne flutes ready for sparkling cider were in hand, when I realized I had forgotten one thing...the bottle opener!

After a moment of panic and disappointment, innovation came. Nothing was going to spoil this celebration. Silently praying, I scanned the surroundings and saw a group sitting off in the distance. I had a good feeling they might come to my rescue. It was a long shot, we were in a park with no alcoholic beverages in sight, but I asked anyway, and they delivered the coolest credit card-size bottle opener ever. The problem mixed with prayer and hope-filled action brought about the solution. In minutes, their glitter flutes were full; laughter and sparkling cider abounded.

That could only have been a fraction of the emotion Mary felt. She knew the hours of preparation that went into creating a place to celebrate life, love, family, and abundance. As a Jewish momma, she knew wedding feasts call for an abundance of wine, and she did not want her friend's celebration to end. Possibly, a more subtle truth stirred in her heart: in God's presence is the fullness of joy, and she knew she stood in the very presence of God. He was in attendance!

Whatever the motivation, I know there was an element of practicality and spiritual significance that fueled her prompts. She knew there was a problem. She didn't pray to Father God, but walked over to Jesus and spoke about the need. With the wine completely gone, Jesus knew she didn't just want Him to hear the problem; she was inviting Him into the solution – or better yet, to *be* the solution.

Mary knew His ability to do impossible things. Jesus knew He would do miracles, heal the sick, raise the dead, and bring abundant life to those who would believe, but hadn't been given a green light. He was waiting for another time. Mary saw a place where a breakthrough could happen because "nothing is impossible with God" (Luke 1:37 NIV). Her goal in approaching Jesus was not to beg nor manipulate, but to open a space that God could not deny: higher thinking birthed from faith.

Telling the servants to follow His instruction, Mary positioned everyone to listen to His voice. She created expectations greater than their imagination. Heaven's resources touched the earth, and the best wine was created from clay jars filled with water. What Mary saw in the unseen reality gave a platform for Jesus to reveal His power.

Partnering with God's resources leads to abundance. Simple obedience mixed with the supernatural makes miracles happen in everyday situations. This story illustrates the profound way that God can create and call into existence from nothing. Don't be afraid to pause and let that sink in for a minute. He creates out of nothing. God did it during creation when He spoke and called light into existence to contrast the darkness. Jesus did it years later when He called into a dark tomb of decay for Lazarus to *awake*. In that moment, life was created (recreated) from death. There are many stories of God making incredible things from nothing.

Jesus wants to BE the way, the truth, and the abundant life you need (John 14:6). Jesus IS the gateway we can enter if we want to experience life, freedom, and satisfaction. He has come to *"give you everything in abundance, more than you expect — life in its fullness until you overflow"* (John 10:9-10 TPT).

What dark or dead places in your story would you like to see God move into? What areas of your heart feel dried up? What areas would you like to invite God to *be* and *do* what only He can? Sometimes embracing what God does for you is the best thing you can do for Him. You, too, can open up heavens so God can move. Higher thinking enables promotion. Moving and raising our mindsets to a higher realm opens places in our everyday lives where unexplainable things can take place.

God can create things in our lives even when we think there is no hope. God's ability far exceeds our wildest imaginations, and we don't have to stop dreaming or believing (see Eph 3:20). We have access to a higher perspective which gives us a platform to launch from. This transforms our thinking and ultimately our behavior. The attitudes we begin to formulate from the time spent in possibility affect how we act and how we advance.

Clinging to God's faithfulness allows us to access the high places,
so we can better occupy the land.

Questions and Reflections
...to ponder on your way to possibilities!

➤What do you think about the following statement? "Promises from God require us to lean into intimacy to see breakthroughs come."

➤What steps will you make to position your thoughts higher?

➤What is God saying to you through this verse? "Fix your heart on the promises of God, and you will dwell in the land, feasting on his faithfulness" (Psalm 37:3-4 TPT).

➤If "perseverance and obedience are like a well-worn path that opens our hearts and situations to receive the miracle," then what steps can you take to persevere and obey God's voice?

➤What "challenges, opinions, judgments, hurt, grief, and fleshly desires" do you need to put under our feet? How does this involve faith and expectation?

9

SEED-SIZED FAITH

ATTITUDE IS where we work out on the ground what we have attained in the high places. Everyday action and reaction show what we are made of. If we were a tree, our attitudes would be the fruit that makes up what kind of tree we are. Our fruit displays our identity. But long before the ripe apple or orange appears on the tree, there is a blossom to signal what is coming. The bud becomes a flower and eventually becomes the product we can eat and give to others. If we back up another few steps, we know that the tree must first have branches, leaves, and a root system. The structures within biology demand a process, and God determined that even before the branches, leaves, and roots there would be a seed.

If our lives fit into this analogy, we see that the attitudes we display reveal our identity. They are defined by us. However, long before our attitudes surface and become either good or bad fruit, there is a process that involves branches, leaves, roots, and initially, seeds. Just as a plant must walk through stages in a process in order to grow and become the plant it is meant to be, there are many points in our journey, down various roads and paths, that will work within us who we are destined to be. Remember, it's not just about the final destination, it's about the process and progress we make along the way towards our destiny.

Identity is a major component in this journey. Identity begins with a small unit (a seed) which brings forth life. This object is able to develop identity and cause growth. The identity can transform a small, hard object into a large, strong, alive entity which not only sustains life but helps support it. It all starts with a seed: an object of reproduction and a source of food.

THE MOUNTAIN

It was a Monday in January, and I was thousands of miles away from my home, my children, and my husband. I had left all my most precious beings to travel across the globe to a remote part of the world with an amazing group of people. Looking back on this trip, I can see how one of the legs of my journey marked me for life. This trip wasn't a vacation. It wasn't just about sightseeing or destinations. It was about carrying truth to the uttermost parts of the earth.

On this day, I was with an incredible team venturing out into a quiet village. We seemed so out of place, a tall white man and short white woman walking down the road with huge smiles. I don't think they had ever seen this sight. Yet there we were, ready to share our story of hope and freedom. Along with our interpreter, our team set off down the road to talk to a family in a nearby home. After having such a rich morning, we were full and expectant for the next thing God was going to do. We had already shared with so many about Jesus' love, and we had watched them confess their sins and receive His forgiveness, making Jesus their Lord. We were blown away by the encounters we had with these sweet people, and we felt so privileged to see lives experience freedom because of the message of the Gospel.

Arriving at the next house, we were greeted in the front yard by a man leading an ox around in circles. At first glance and being from a very western culture that doesn't see things like this on a regular basis, I was intrigued. The whole team was mesmerized, and we watched the man lead the animal around what appeared to be a threshing floor. There were branches laid out in a huge circle, and as the man walked the ox around it, the weight of the ox and the stomping motion shook loose the branches' seeds. I bent down and scooped up a handful of the seeds that had been shaken free.

The hundreds of seeds I held in my hand were so tiny, and my mind immediately went to the story in the Bible where Jesus talks about a very small seed. In this story, Jesus tells the crowd that if they would have faith as small as a mustard seed, they could speak to a mountain, tell it to move, and it would. I turned to my team with excitement and said, I think God is trying to get our attention! Here I was watching a shaking taking place to loosen this smallest of seeds, and my heart stirred as the Holy Spirit reminded me of Jesus' picture lesson. Mustard seed-sized faith can make impossible things happen! My heart leapt with joy and faith began to rise in me. I was convinced God had given us that lesson with our natural eyes to prepare our hearts for what He was about to do if we would choose to partner with Him. Faith believes and declares. Jesus said to have faith and tell the mountain to move. My heart had faith, so I asked the Father to show me where our mountain was.

We began speaking with those who had come to listen to our message. Through our translator, we shared our testimony and the message of the Gospel. Tears began to fill their eyes, and they wanted to know the Jesus who had loved them so much to die for their sins. We prayed with them and rejoiced as they chose Jesus.

Then, a lady who was in extreme pain was escorted in. We were told she had once had a tumor, but as a Christian prayed for her, the tumor left. She had experienced healing and believed in Jesus. Shortly after that encounter, the pain was back, and she was paralyzed down half of her body. I sensed the pain was caused by a demonic stronghold (I will explain this later) and that as we prayed, she needed to believe with faith and speak to the mountain. I heard the Holy Spirit whisper to my heart that she needed to renounce her

Hindu gods and claim Jesus as the only God. I explained this to the translator and as we prayed for her, we had her repeat the words God gave me, declaring faith in the One true God and renouncing all other gods. Specific gods came to mind, and with words of faith, we declared their power null and void in her life. We spoke out loud to the mountains (gods) that had held her captive. The powers she had once relied on were cut off from her by her confession of faith in the One true God. With that prayer and that confession, she began to smile. Pain left her body and she was healed! We saw it with our own eyes. She was full of joy, the countenance of her face changed, and she was able to move her arm and leg. The painful, paralyzed side of her body was now free! We spoke to the mountain, and it moved!

WHAT IF

That day, the mustard seed was an invitation to go beyond natural sight into a supernatural realm. My heart saw the natural sign, and then leaned in to view what God wanted to do in the unseen realm of this woman's heart. The small amount of faith, even as tiny as a mustard seed, made the impossible possible! That was the truth Jesus spoke to His disciples after they came up against a demonic spirit tormenting a boy. Seeing this boy having seizures and foaming at the mouth caused fear in the hearts of the village. Scared and full of sorrow, the boy's father asked Jesus for mercy because the disciples couldn't drive the demon out.

First of all, if I was the parent in this situation, I would be doing whatever it took to find an answer, a solution to this problem. My mama bear heart would rise up, and I would vow to keep searching until I could find someone to help my son. Most parents and people would stand up on behalf of a child. Maybe there are things you see happening around you that stir up that justice bone too. What injustices or pain around you (or maybe inside of your own life) are you willing to fight for? This father had that fight, even when those around him didn't.

Jesus saw the unbelief of the crowd, but also saw the seed-sized faith in the eyes of the father. So, He called for the boy to be brought to Him. As soon as the demonic spirit who had possessed the boy saw Jesus, it reacted. The boy began foaming at the mouth and was tossed around by unseen forces. Again, in desperation, the father asks, "If you're able to do something, anything—have compassion on us and help us!" (Mark 9:23 TPT). The next verse hits me at my core. I imagine Jesus looking into the Father's eyes after seeing his son thrashing on the ground, people staring, crowds judging with disgust, and yet with compassion, Jesus responds, "What do you mean 'if'? If you are able to believe, all things are possible to the believer" (Mark 9:33 TPT). There it is! Two little letters describe enough faith to move mountains. *If* you have faith as small as a mustard seed, *if* you can believe with baby step faith, then there are endless possibilities.

The small amount of belief that said *if* God was willing, the entire childhood of trauma, the life of bondage, or the multiple years of the same behaviors and obstacles could be eradicated because of the healing power of Jesus. With weariness, sleeplessness, and countless stories of disappointment, the father cries out, "Help my *seed-sized faith!*" No excuses, without justifying his doubt, and without explaining all they had tried, he simply states, *if* there is any part of my heart or mindset that is stuck in unbelief, take it from me. I want all things that are possible, not what I see now.

Can you relate? My hands are raised, and I know the heartache of watching someone you love go through a debilitating disease. I have seen the effects of bondage on life, including years of chronic pain. I have watched loved ones fight mental anguish. But I want to pause and say that one encounter with Jesus can change it all. We see it in this story in the Gospels, I have experienced it in my own heart, and have seen it with my own eyes in the little village next to the threshing floor. Simply put, the threshing floor is a place where the usable seed is separated from what can't be used.

THRESH IT OUT

The shaking that took place as the ox stomped his way in circles is essentially what life's circumstances can provide for us. Has disease hit your house? Has there been a loss of job or danger to your finances? Has the chaos of politics, rumors of wars, or fear of freedom being lost caused a shaking to take place? Are there places and spaces in your world that are being ground down and threshed? If after reading any of those statements you feel a big yes coming from your mouth, then rest assured. With the shaking comes hundreds of mustard seeds that just need to be sown into the soil of your heart and the soil of your situations.

With so many opportunities, small faith can produce big and lasting results. There are opportunities to sow seeds of faith daily. Even when our eyes can't see and our circumstances can't reflect it, we can have a belief in God who is able. We can make a declaration stating it's time to leave behind the ways of the past, the philosophies of the world, and the limiting mindsets. It is time to renounce our old gods or things we put our trust in. It is time to leave behind the things that hold our attention and choose to partner with the One who can take the *ifs* in our hearts and move mountains in our midst.

The boy's life was changed when he was brought to Jesus. Can we bring our disappointments to Jesus? Can you hand over your children to Jesus? Do your family or finances need transformation from Jesus? Part of the journey we are on is learning how mixing our faith with the transforming power of Jesus brings freedom! So, what are the places and spaces in your heart that need freedom? Have anxiety and fear bound you up so tight that you have lost peace? Has worry and depression taken over your thoughts so that some days you barely want to get out of bed? What is God shaking in your heart right now as you read these words?

Be encouraged; with the shaking, there are now seeds available to plant. There are many *if* emotions, thoughts, or beliefs that we can present to the One who transforms. Our faith, as small as it is, can be like a tangible seed we give to God each day. We have a tangible substance (faith) that is able to develop identity and cause growth in our lives. Just like a seed can become a large, strong, living, breathing tree, faith is able to transform areas of destruction and death into something strong and life giving. It starts with a seed. Faith is the object of reproduction which allows God to reproduce life into our situations.

THE GUARANTEE

So, what does faith look like in our everyday life? To answer that, can I give you a few facts? Hebrews 11 defines faith for us, and includes the Greek word *hupostasis.*[7] It means "to place or set under," referring to something that is foundational. Further explained, it's the assurance, the guarantee of reality. Faith can also be the thing that gives a reason to endure and stand under the weight of the opposition, with security under our feet. It is referred to as a "substance of things hoped for, and the evidence of things not seen" (see Heb 11:1). It is the foundational, underlying truth and promise of God's nature. Some view it like the foundation of a building. It is the very core of what we can place our hope on.

In Greek culture, it was also used as a legal term to represent the document that showed proof of ownership. It was the piece of paper that we refer to today as a title deed. It names the things we have access, authority, or legal right to. Faith is assurance and proof of ownership of things we may not have right in front of us yet or may be unseen. It guarantees that what we are talking about is ours; it belongs to us.

Faith is the thing that gives us access to what God has bought for us. He paid for your salvation; He has given you freedom in Christ. Faith is the guarantee or reality that all of heaven's resources belong to us because of Christ Jesus. In a way, faith is the key that takes us into the storehouses of heaven and unlocks possibilities. It makes the impossible possible, allowing us unlimited access to everything God has for us. It is not just a theory; it's tangible proof that you have the right and authority to have what God has promised you. That is why you can ask, in His name, according to what He has already spoken, and it is yours. Your faith is the title deed that proves it!

So, what has God promised you? What word has He spoken to your heart, in your dreams, or from His Word that you know is His promise to you? Those promises are the foundation to put your hope on. That is what you build upon. Whatever He has said He will do, you attach your proof of ownership to that! He has given you the title because He is a good Father. He has paid for it and gave it (in faith) to you. All you must do is refer to it as the authority and proof that God's promise for you is abundant life. He promises to give you a future full of hope, not one of harm or destruction. That is how I picture hope. It is the thing we are waiting for and anticipating. Hope is the thing we talk about with future tense. Faith, on the other hand, is the belief that we have it already! It may not be in front of us, and we may not be able to see it with our own eyes yet, but we have received the title deed. We hold it and it proves our right to what we can't see yet.

Here is a good place to stop and identify some of the promises that God has given you. Take a moment to go back through your memories or your Bible and see the verses you have highlighted. Maybe you have kept a journal or received a note from a friend. What are the encouragements that you hold onto when life gets hectic and you need peace or hope? I like to keep them written down so I can go back and look at them. I make a list or have a document on my computer with lists of words, promises, and verses that I know will bring hope, encouragement, and courage to keep pressing through when I can't see the change yet.

Let's put them in front of us as a daily reminder so we don't forget what we are believing and fighting for. They are the *why* behind our walk. They provide the reason for living in a faith-filled reality. The early Israelites had a tangible way to do this. They were told to, "Tie them on your arms and wear them on your foreheads as a reminder" (Deut 6:8 GNT). This challenge to remember came immediately after God instructed His people with important truths they were to live by. Their obedience in remembering and living by these principles were what would take them into new land to occupy it! Be encouraged, we are a people who are called to move forward and take ground, and with authority from the King, we can occupy it!

We will discuss *occupying* more in depth later, but for now, be encouraged that God's promises give us hope and tangible access into the more we are believing for. We don't have to wonder *if* we can get there, and we don't have to worry we aren't allowed to go. We can proceed with promises that give us permission. In fact, faith does not worry or strive. It is confident, knowing we have access to all of God's promises, permissions, and provisions. We don't have to strive, be anxious, or try to manufacture it. We can rest in this knowledge: whatever God said He would do, be, or give us for a situation, He will. Faith is confidence that we have what He has spoken.

Promises are the why behind our walk.
They provide the reason for living in a faith-filled reality.

Questions and Reflections
...to ponder on your way to possibilities!

➤What fruit is displayed by (the tree of) your life?

➤What mountain (situation) in your life needs to be moved? In which area do you need to activate seed-sized faith?

➤What do you think about Jesus' words? "If you are able to believe, all things are possible to the believer" (Mark 9:33 TPT).

➤What are the places and spaces in your heart that need freedom? What do you need to bring to Jesus?

➤What promises from God do you need to see as your legal right? How has He given you proof of ownership over those areas?

10

NOT ORNAMENTAL

Eyes closed, my mind was deep in thought as I breathed in the cool air. Then, he sat on me. Yes, he jumped right on me; the entire weight of his being pressing down on my lap. It was uncomfortable but comical. My affectionate, miniature (in name only) schnauzer thinks I am his favorite person. His only goal in life, besides catching lizards or birds, is to be with me. When he can land on my lap and turn Rigor Mortis on me so he doesn't have to be moved, it's his best day. This dog loves me and loves to be with me. In reality, he is always with me which is not an exaggeration. He lays under my chair, on my lap, or behind my back serving as lumbar support. He knows how to abide and remain.

Abide is an old English word, one we hear in old literature or verses from the Bible. It is not part of our everyday vernacular, but it's a rich word to explore. Though the modern English meaning has to do with tolerating something or accepting the rule or law, the old English definition has a deeper significance. This underused word means "to remain with, dwell with, stay with, and wait under."[8] The origin of this meaning is also seen in the Greek word *meno,*[9] which can be found in one of my favorite chapters in the Bible: the story of a vine in John chapter 15.

ABIDING PRODUCES FRUIT

Jesus was an incredible storyteller, and I love reading through the parables and analogies He used when talking to one or many. He tells a story to His followers and weaves the picture of a vine full of branches throughout His teaching. The chapter begins with a master gardener cutting off branches that aren't producing fruit and pruning the ones that are bearing fruit so they will produce even more (see John 15).

Jesus relates His story to the listeners when He explains that He is the vine and those who follow Him, loving Him and choosing Him as their life source, are the branches. One of the main points He addresses is how the branches attached to the vine have the ability to produce fruit. This is where the word *abide* is used. Those who abide (remain in, dwell with, or stay connected to) will see fruit in their lives. If we remain (abide) in Jesus and He remains in us, then we will have a constant source of life coming in and flowing out of us. We can be branches that produce good things!

I never knew there was so much involved in growing plants...until I tried. Tending a garden, especially with the intent to produce fruit, is not a task for the faint of heart. Without knowledge, you assume, you water, and let them grow. I have found out the hard way over the years that there are many things a plant needs and many variables to their success. Growth depends on the right amount of light and nutrients in their soil. Factors like drainage and the amount of water are crucial. All of these can accelerate or deter growth, not to mention prevent or produce fruit.

Attitudes are the fruit that is produced from the soil of our circumstances. In life, maintenance is required to grow and produce attitudes that resemble good fruit. Like with the master gardener, there will be steps we take in every situation to either remove things or provide better soil, light, and proper water and nutrients for growth. Similar to pruning branches to remove the dead foliage, we will need to address attitudes and atmospheres. The beliefs and motives behind our attitudes will allow for the new growth we want to see in our hearts, relationships, and circumstances.

Jesus could have picked any example of any crop or plant, but He chose a vineyard that exists to produce wine. I have heard it said that superior wine requires superior grapevines. It all starts with the vine. Good wine came about because of good fruit. Good fruit is produced by a good vine, and if Jesus is that vine, it means we will produce well if we are *in Christ*. By living planted, rooted, and established in Jesus, we have the ability to bear fruit. We don't cause the fruit to come. We can't manufacture fruit. The fruit comes because we (the branches) are attached to the life source and have chosen to abide there. From that place, fruit develops

NOT ORNAMENTAL FRUIT

There are many different types of vines, plants, and trees. Some are full of color and vibrancy. The flowers they produce are incredible to look at and attract birds and bees. However, many that would wow us are just ornamental. They do not produce edible fruit; they are just for show. They are spectacular, have their place in our gardens, and help preserve the insect and bird population. However, they cannot be eaten.

It is no mistake that Jesus' lesson on abiding referenced vines. This picture is all about root systems, growth, pruning, and life. Not to mention, a vine produces grapes which are fruit that can be eaten. It is no coincidence that Jesus compared our lives to the grape vine. We exist to produce consumable fruit. God designed our life and relationship with Him to produce fruit that can be eaten by us and given out to others – to nourish and provide sustenance for our journey.

Though a vineyard exists to produce wine, I love how grapes can also be eaten right as they are plucked. No preparation, peeling, or cooking is needed. They can be given away or enjoyed right from the plant. Also, the fruit of this vine can also be pressed, processed, and aged to produce wine. Many variables will affect the result. The type of barrel or vessel, the temperature or climate of the space, the fermenting process, the crushing, and the aging...I can't even imagine the vast knowledge and care required to make wine. Like the grape, there are parts of our journey that will allow our fruit to be instant nourishment. There will also be parts to our journey that requires us to take our attitudes and let them be refined through the process, aged to maturity before they are perfected. Remember, our journey is not all about the immediate. There are many aspects of our process that take time and require us to not only abide in Him but yield to the Holy Spirit in order to produce what the Gardener is after.

This is an important moment. The lightbulb just went on for some of you. There are parts of your life that need time, space, revelation, and maturity to make you ready. As you read this, you already feel like the everyday demands of life require you to hand out what you have. You feel the urgency of those who want to pick the fruit right out of your hands, to consume it immediately and leave you empty. Your season may be one of tending to the immediate, or it may be one of development. In those times of handing out or holding on, allow God to show you how abiding impacts maturing and the quality of what is produced. No one likes to be handed unripe fruit when what they really need is the satisfaction that comes from a juicy bite.

In the busy moments of life's demands, there is a way to ask God for greater revelation. He speaks. We listen. He reveals to our hearts the areas of our internal world that are in process. Your belief system might be getting pressed right now. You are figuring out how your heart and head connect. You are wondering if you have been spending too much time trying to make your life beautiful and presentable, but you realize now that the fruit you've been growing is ornamental. Don't be discouraged. It's not too late. You may just be realizing how the time and effort you have spent was focused on making everyone else happy and pollinating those around you. Your heart is awakened to want more. You want your life to be like a tree whose pollen can be carried to the next, but you also want to produce deliciously edible fruit. There is still time.

Colossians 1:10-11 says, "We pray that you would walk in the ways of true righteousness, pleasing God in every good thing that you do. Then you will become fruit-bearing branches, yielding to his life, and maturing in the rich experience of knowing God in his fullness." There it is! That can become your life mission. Our goal is to journey well, living in a way that is pleasing to Him. And if we look deeper than that, there is a reason behind our purpose. We were created to be loved and loved. This involves abiding. The product that comes from our intimate abiding love is consumable, life-giving, and juicy fruit. We have a say in how our journey goes, and no matter what season we are in, we can posture our lives to abide. From that place, attached to the giver of life, we have clarity and strength to walk pleasing to God, producing fruit instead of living ornamental lives just for show!

GIVE IT AWAY

When my kids were young, we enjoyed our play dates at a park, someone's house, or even the beach to have a little fun in the sun. It was a great chance to get out of the house and foster community, especially during the years I homeschooled my kids. Yes, I was one of those crazy moms who enjoyed being with her kids and teaching them things! I still love being with them all these years later. They are great kids!

One sunny day, we packed up our sack lunch and set off for the day. There was a park right next to the bay, and so we could enjoy the sand, the water, and the playground. We were ready to enjoy a day of splashing in the water and hanging out.

At lunch time, we unpacked our food. As I reached for the bag of oranges, my eight-year-old son's eyes began to sparkle. He asked if he could take some food to the homeless man we saw when we arrived. To be honest, my heart and mind went racing. I wasn't sure if I should feel panic or pride that my son wanted to walk up to a stranger and engage with him to offer him food. Not knowing his mental or emotional state, I quickly paused and prayed. Then, I felt the nudge from the Holy Spirit to partner with my son's compassion and take the man some oranges.

With every step, I felt my heart fluctuating back and forth between two questions. The first being, *what am I doing?* After all, I could possibly be walking my son and I into a dangerous situation. The second question being, *Holy Spirit, what do I need to know?* I have learned that in every situation, especially those prompted by the Father or Holy Spirit, there is security, direction, and provision if we will keep our hearts abiding in Him. Stepping out on our own or outside of what God is doing can create feelings of being alone. But when our hearts remain focused on His voice, words, and heart, our abiding gives freedom, permission, and peace.

My son and I talked on the way over. We prayed that God would give us the right words to say and grace to know what this divine appointment was all about. We postured our attitude to be dependent on His guidance. As we got closer, God's love and compassion, the same love and compassion that started us on this long walk, rose up inside. Smiles formed on our faces, and we greeted him asking if we could talk to him. He agreed.

We introduced ourselves and told him we noticed him as we sat down for lunch and felt God's love prompt us to offer him some food. He was grateful. God gave me a few things to tell him, and we asked him some questions about his life. Then, my son asked if there was anything he would like us to pray about. He mentioned he was out of work, but actively looking for a job. He could do handyman things and would like us to pray for him. We prayed with hope, faith, and a heart full of compassion. We were confident God had set up this meeting and was going to move in his life. We spoke words of life over him and blessed him, then went our way.

Our attitudes had chosen love and compassion over comfort. We kept our hearts in Christ and stayed full of peace, even though some might have experienced anxiety or fear. Words and actions are not for show. We didn't go talk to the homeless man so everyone on the beach would be impressed by our act of kindness. It was an overflow of compassion that my son carries. In fact, while I was pregnant with him, it was one of the things I prayed into existence! I prayed he would have that trait of compassion – a soft heart towards Jesus and others. Compassion is part of his DNA, and the fruit of his life fed a man on the street that day.

Abiding is directly connected to our attitudes. How and if we remain in Christ determines how we behave. The way we think, our internal belief, is reflected in our behavior. That day, we not only fed a homeless man, but provided space for him to receive spiritual food. Our words and actions nourished his spirit, his soul, and his body. The fruit we produce is not ornamental. It is to be consumed by people for their encouragement, giving them hope, joy, and peace.

A couple of weeks later, my friend was back at that park with her kids. She recognized the same man we had given fruit to. She talked to him and found out that shortly after we prayed with him, he met a lady in the apartment nearby. She needed a handyman and gave him a temporary job. He was able to work, make a little money, and most of all see that God cared about his needs. He was loved by an unseen God because a small boy thought it prudent to take him some oranges.

CONSUMABLE FRUIT

Jesus is intentional. He doesn't just tell stories to tell them. There is always truth and a deeper meaning attached. Again, I love how He used the picture of a grapevine, because wine often references the Holy Spirit. It is a picture of what He does in our lives; how He empowers us, gives us boldness, and fills us with joy. It is a symbol of abundance and God pouring out His blessing on us. In many places in Scripture, God talks about the containers of wine overflowing because of God's provision and about our need to be filled with the Holy Spirit!

There is also a theme that runs throughout the Bible of the fruit that comes from the relationship to the Spirit. It's "divine love in all its varied expressions: joy that overflows, peace that subdues, patience that endures, kindness in action, a life full of virtue, faith that prevails, gentleness of heart, and strength of spirit. Never set the law above these qualities, for they are meant to be limitless" (Galatians 5:22 TPT). The *more* we are going after has no limits in the Spirit. He is full, abundant, and provides everything we need.

This incredible list gives us hope that in every circumstance He will provide. We don't have to be afraid that we are incapable, unqualified, or unprepared. His love is with us for relationships that have hurt us and need forgiveness. His peace is available as we face the fears of parenting, ministry, and financial uncertainty. His patience is accessible as we wait to see the healing come. Joy, kindness, and gentleness are not just present in little amounts, but in limitless supply. His nature and character in us are the fruit we produce. As we stay connected and learn what it means to encounter His Spirit with intentional desire, we begin to understand the difference between doing and being. Being in Him helps us regulate our life. Abiding in Him allows us to leave behind an ornamental life and go after a life that produces fruit worth consuming.

Our lives exist to produce consumable fruit.

Questions and Reflections
...to ponder on your way to possibilities!

➤Do you see yourself as a producer of edible fruit?

➤Do you relate more to being in a season of fresh fruit or pressed fruit?

➤What does the following verse say about your life? Colossians 1:10-11: "We pray that you would walk in the ways of true righteousness, pleasing God in every good thing that you do. Then you will become fruit-bearing branches, yielding to his life, and maturing in the rich experience of knowing God in his fullness."

➤What would others say about the fruit you offer? What is in the DNA of your fruit?

➤Do you believe this statement? "The *more* we are going after has no limits in the Spirit. He is full, abundant, and provides everything we need."

11

CHOOSE YOUR WORLDS

AUTHOR CHARLES R. Swindoll once stated, "I am convinced that life is 10% what happens to me and 90% of how I react to it."[10] Our attitude, or 90% of what we define as life choices, is directly affected by our reaction to issues, circumstances, and difficulties. These choices affect our internal world. Our internal world then affects our external world, and ultimately those around us.

Our actions mirror our internal temperature. If we are at peace internally, we tend to walk out that peace in circumstances. It is harder for your face and body to reflect the opposite of how you're feeling. When we get angered by something someone has done to us, it takes self-control not to react based on their actions or attitudes. Every step requires us to choose our attitude. If we choose good fruit, there is a place of internal rest we can go back to. Emotions should not dictate our attitudes...where we remain should!

WHAT STATE DO YOU LIVE IN

I love to travel. There is a level of adventure that I appreciate. I am not one of those wild, try anything type of people. Being somewhat reserved, I do enjoy beautiful places, cultures, and a little bit of spontaneity. There was a point in my journey when I was a mom of three kids under the age of two. You would imagine that was an adventure in itself. I was good at planning ahead to avoid some mishaps that could have caused cliffs to fall off. But no matter how much you plan, there are always unforeseen things.

One vacation, we took a trip from one coast of the U.S. to the other. We sat at the gate, and then boarded our flight with three tiny kids. I can only imagine the people watching us board the plane. If they had never prayed, they probably started that day, praying we didn't sit next to them! My husband and I are a good team, and that day we divided to conquer. We knew what each kid needed and what things could possibly set them off. So, with sippy cups, goldfish, books, toys, and prayers fully stocked up, we began our adventure.

Our three little ones were doing great. They were enjoying the flight. The four-month-old twins were happy to sit on Mom and Dad's lap, and our two-year-old was content and asking questions with that sweet little voice of his. The people sitting around us began to relax when they realized our kids were going to stay calm and let them enjoy their flight.

Maybe you have been on a similar flight with babies or vocal passengers nervous to fly. We have all seen them. The more uncomfortable they get, the more vocal. No matter who is talking, they get cranky, which makes the flight difficult for all those within eyesight and ear shot. Whether a screaming child or an angry passenger, they make sure everyone else knows what a difficult time they are having.

Fortunately for me and everyone on our flight, my children were content and calm, despite any turbulence or unruly passengers. As they sat on Mom and Dad's lap, fully loved and fully cared for, they stayed in peace. They remained calm – no tears, no problems, no fear. Just rest.

Not every person remains in that state. We could all say we have seen that passenger (or maybe been that passenger) who has let fear and anxiety rob them of peace. Our internal state affects the external state. What we nurture and partner within the inner places will quickly be revealed on our face by our words or through our actions.

The internal state of my kids was peaceful because they felt secure where they sat. Their internal temperature was at rest, allowing them to sleep, eat, and play as their laps remained planted on ours. They were abiding in the safety of mom and dad's arms.

The question we must constantly ask ourselves is *how often do we let our internal panic and unsettledness take us out of a place of security?* It is easy to let the stresses of life, the things we don't have control over, and the uncertainties set us off. We either choose to fall or allow ourselves to be escorted out of peace by emotions, frustrations, or even unmet expectations. When we do this, our internal world is exposed because of circumstances. When things don't go our way, we can either choose to stay planted in the security of our Heavenly Father or get knocked out of our place of peace.

POWER OF PEACE

God often does things first in the natural, and then applies or reveals the spiritual significance. He also shows physical representations of what was going on internally. Jesus and His disciples had many long days of serving people. They had put up with crowds and functioned with limited sleep and food. The stories don't always share details about the state of their mind and bodies, but if you read the portions before, you'll usually see they have been serving lots of people with needs. They watched disease, sickness, and demonic activity be turned from faith to miracles. You would think they were always on a spiritual high after what they had experienced and been part of.

In one story, Jesus tells the disciples they are all going to cross the lake. They are in a bit of a transition period. They are leaving behind the land, the authority, and the assignment they were fulfilling and heading to *the other side.* Getting on a boat at this point was kind of like the airplane ride we took from one coast to the other. Here, the disciples stepped aboard knowing this time of travel and transition would reposition them for their next thing.

Jesus knew they might need to see with their natural eyes what was taking place in their internal spaces. As they head out, Jesus makes Himself comfortable for this leg of the journey. The disciples follow Him on board but don't follow Him into a state of rest. Two Gospels describe what happened next as furious! As Jesus slept, a storm came upon the lake, causing waves to come over the boat. If you have ever been in a boat, a kayak, or even on a pool float, you know that the last thing you want to happen is for a storm to hit and huge ferocious waves to come over your flotation device! In that type of moment, the story tells us Jesus kept on sleeping, completely at rest, while the furious storm rages around Him.

The book of Mark describes a scene where the waves were breaking over the boat, "so that it was nearly swamped," and Jesus was, "sleeping on a cushion" (Mark 4:37-38 NIV). What a great image. It doesn't sound like Jesus nodded off due to exhaustion. It sounds like He made Himself comfortable on a cushion, ready to enjoy a peaceful sleep. We don't know whether God gave Him insight into the coming storm or not, but we do know He postured himself in rest, knowing He could sleep and be at peace because He lived in a place of security with the Father.

In the text, we see that though Jesus had prepared for peace, the disciples have not followed suit. They are not sleeping. They are not at rest and are not at peace. Running over, the disciples frantically wake Jesus, pleading for Him to save them. First, kudos to them for recognizing Jesus is able to save them. I don't want to skip over that part. However, their next reaction, most of us can relate to. The external problem either messed with their internal state or revealed it. In my opinion, they either allowed the storm to be the situation that pulled them out of safety into panic, or they never were in a true place of peace.

I can relate to both. I know there have been times in my life when I started out in a good place; my heart was fixed and my confidence in

God's ability to save me was never in question. What ruins it for us is that we don't remain there. We don't reside there. We don't allow faith to be what keeps us in trust...which keeps us in peace.

If we are going to talk this much about abiding, then we need to pause here. True abiding, remaining, and ultimately rest requires trust. Trust is not an option. True rest, remaining in that place of peace or confidence in God's saving and safety, demands trust. The disciples knew God was able to save them, but they didn't realize they could abide or live in that state. They understood that in life and in a boat, there would be storms. What they didn't realize is that their internal temperature can remain in peace no matter what. They had confidence in God's ability, but didn't understand how to trust Him with their inner world.

How many times and places in our journey do we acknowledge God is able to do things for others, just not for us? We make statements that He can do it for you or how He did it for me, but we don't abide in that practical knowledge that He can do it again. Disappointment is real. There are times when it *worked before,* but it doesn't feel like it is working now. That is when I realize it's not about formulas; it's about a relationship.

Former actress and movement leader Lauren Hasson says, "The biggest gift is to recognize where I don't know him yet."[11] When we have faced disappointments or haven't experienced Him in particular areas, we don't have to let our internal space become occupied with fear. We can choose peace or love or joy...whatever He wants to be for us in those unfamiliar places in our life. The key is to be aware, stay alert, and press into Him. Stay so close that we set up a residence in God. No matter what we face, good or bad, our internal state can look to see who He will be for us.

Trusting who God is looks like confidence that says His love doesn't leave us, even when disappointment, rejection, or unmet expectations come. Trust looks like assurance that God's goodness will be what I need in the middle of the storm, even if the storm continues to rage around me. Rest comes when we can stay planted on the promises He has made us because we choose to be certain that His words are living and active; His words create life from nothing. There is a great assurance that our Heavenly Father can calm storms whether internal or external.

That airplane ride taught me the importance of staying in peace. The state we choose to live in becomes the difference between calm and distraught. That is how we maintain our internal state and have our behavior in response be the fruit of the Spirit we talked about earlier. Abiding is crucial to having the right attitude in every circumstance. Having these attitudes is how we choose which worlds we live in as we move forward. They position us for what we long for most: intimacy.

No matter what we face, good or bad, our internal state can look to see who He will be for us.

Questions and Reflections
...to ponder on your way to possibilities!

~

➤What kind of internal state do you live in most of the time? When the storms of life make waves around you, where do you run? What do you run to?

➤How often do you let your internal panic and unsettledness take you out of a place of security or peace?

➤Have you ever thought of the following? "God is able to do things for others, just not for me." Why do you think you believe this?

➤Do you agree that "true abiding, remaining, and ultimately rest requires trust"? Why or why not?

➤Why do the attitudes we choose determine which worlds we live in as we move forward? What does the following statement mean? "They position us for what we long for most: intimacy."

Part three

THRONE ROOM
ENCOUNTERS

12

AN ENCOUNTER WITH JESUS

No matter the season of our journey, we must find time and space away from the hurry, distractions, and demands. With intention we need to separate ourselves from daily life to quiet our hearts. Intentional expectation paired with silence gives space for God to speak. Jesus knew this to be true and modeled it for us. He often left the hustle of the city or ministry to go off by Himself to pray. He went up a mountainside, hid in a house, and even got in a boat to leave the crowds behind. I imagine some of this time was to recharge, but I know some of it was to speak to the Father and listen.

This habit is necessary for our hearts to be healed, empowered, and commissioned. It is our responsibility, like Jesus, to know when to be in it and when to remove ourselves from it for a time of refreshing. Whether we set time aside or the Holy Spirit jumps in and intervenes, there must be a place and space for these encounters. No one can encounter the Father, Jesus, or Holy Spirit and walk away unchanged.

The word *encounter* is defined as "an unexpected experience, or casual meeting."[12] God is all about encounters. He longs to reveal opportunities to experience Him and deepen relationships. It's true;

there are many accounts in the Bible of a time when God suddenly or unexpectedly showed up and revealed Himself in an experience. I see examples in both the Old and New Testament which support this definition.

One encounter happened to a man named Saul while on his way to Damascus. With a letter from the priest in his hand and anger in his heart, he carried this letter that gave him power to arrest anyone who followed Jesus Christ of Nazareth. Out in the middle of the road, in between water breaks and determined steps, God interrupted Saul's journey with a light beaming down from heaven. The light was so profound and powerful that Saul got on his knees, and then heard an audible voice speaking to him!

I can imagine Saul trying to shield his eyes from the intense shine. Hands over his face, knees weak, and heart racing, he hears the voice ask, "Why do you persecute me?" (Act 9:4 NIV). That seems like a reasonable question directed to this man, because at this point in his life, Saul has persecuted many. The problem is Saul doesn't even know who is speaking. Hoping to gain some understanding of what is going on, Saul listens as Jesus identifies Himself as the one being persecuted. Stunned that God would show up, Saul, now blind, is told to get up and go into the city. No details. No long conversation. Saul is simply told to rise and then commissioned with a task. It is an incredible encounter, and I encourage you to read the entire story.

One of the amazing things about this story is that it doesn't end with one encounter. While Saul and his traveling companions shake in fear on their way to Damascus, the same Jesus who spoke with a reverberating voice and appeared with brilliant light went to quietly encounter a man named Ananias. This time, God showed up in a vision, telling Ananias to go to a specific place. The meaning of this word for vision tells us it was a supernatural sight from God. Using pictures and speaking words to Ananias in his imagination, God tells him where to find Saul. God instructed Ananias to place his hands on Saul and restore his sight.

Two encounters: one audible, affecting natural sight, and one supernatural, bringing information to mind and spiritual eyes. Both encounters revealed God's power and God's heart. Both men walked away with clear instruction and a deep stirring in their heart to see more.

If you were in Ananias' shoes, you might be scared off because of the stories about this man who persecutes followers of Jesus. Ananias adamantly retells God what he has heard about this man. As if God needed that reminder, God repeats His instruction and further clarifies Saul's true identity. God removes any doubt by saying, "This man is my chosen instrument to carry my name before the Gentiles and their kings and before the people of Israel" (Acts 9:15 NIV). Yes, this man who once persecuted Christians has been labeled by God as an instrument to carry God's name. His identity and everything God has destined him for has been exposed to the world.

God doesn't just show up with a smile during this exchange. This encounter for both Saul and Ananias is a weighty one. God spoke to both men to facilitate an extreme transformation. Both needed to hear and see the Father's heart for this situation. God wanted to reveal to Saul that he was made for more. The Father wanted Ananias to know there is redemption in the name of Jesus, and before He calls and commissions, there is a choosing. God chose Saul, who later would become Paul, an apostle who facilitated a movement! Now that's an encounter!

Not every encounter comes out of the blue. There are sudden moments like we just saw, but more often God comes as a response to our hunger. Posturing our hearts, minds, and bodies in humility, desperation, or desire invites the Holy Spirit to come. I imagine it's similar to the pheromones put out by insects and mammals which affect the behavior and physiology of their species. Our intentional pursuit of God releases a type of spiritual pheromone that allures the presence of God. God sees and senses our hunger, and then responds. One of my favorite ways to enter into His presence, while simultaneously posturing myself in hunger, is worship.

Worship can be singing songs to Jesus or about Him. However, worship encompasses so much more. It involves the posture of our heart as it relates to reverence, honor, devotion, and adoration of One we deem higher than ourselves. Our lives, the way we live and love, can be an act of devotion or worship. Adoration is the game changer. It is a posture that opens our hearts and minds to receive.

One day, a phrase was whispered to my heart by the Father as He was inviting me into an encounter. He simply spoke this to my heart: *adoration is a doorway into the heavenlies.* Adoration opened the door of my heart and invited me into a transformational encounter with Jesus.

MY ENCOUNTER WITH THE KING

Alone in my room, I danced and sang with such freedom. I had set aside this moment to enter into a place of worship. So with excitement, I clapped, shouted, and danced unashamedly in the privacy of my home. No eyes watching, no ears listening, except One. In celebration, I raised my voice, giving Him pieces of my heart, my love, and my adoration. Then, the excitement shifted into stillness. I felt the weightiness of love enter the room. It was tangible, though not visible. My heart reached out of my chest, and all I wanted was to be near Him. So, I bowed in response to such majesty. I could feel the majesty. As I knelt before the King, I looked up with tears streaming down my face. I was undone in His goodness.

I saw Jesus in my room. He was there, standing in His Kingly garments, with a crown upon his head, and the train of His robe extended out beyond Him. The sight was magnificent. I had never seen it with my natural eyes before. I had imagined Him as King. I had dreamed about Him as King, but never had I stood before Him where I felt like I could reach out and touch Him. I looked around my room. I could still see it all. To my side was my bed, my dresser, and the light coming in the window from the outside, and there stood the King of Kings. He was larger than a human man, and His being was not bound by my space. He filled the space but was outside of the items I could still see in my room. It was as if He stood there with me in my realm, but He was in another layer of space.

As my eyes glistened with tears, He spoke. His voice was not audible to my natural ears, but could be heard internally in the very depth of my spirit. I could feel the reverberation in my chest. My cells vibrated as He spoke to me saying, "Rise, my daughter." I scrambled to my feet, wanting to do whatever He spoke; there was such love, goodness, and authority behind His words. As I rose, my instinct was to put out my hands. This posture of receiving was natural for me, and so I cupped my hands and extended them. Somehow internally I knew He had something to give me, so I put my hands out ready to receive His gift.

Jesus stood in front of me, and He took off the robe that hung around His neck. He handed the robe to me, putting it around my shoulders. He then placed a ring on my finger. It was shiny and made of pure gold with a ruby in the center. His action confirmed the longing in my heart – that I was precious to Him and loved beyond measure.

Next, He handed me a ring with keys on it. Several keys of different shapes and sizes hung on the metal ring. Internally, I heard my heart respond, "Are these the keys to your Kingdom?" Jesus spoke again to my heart and said, "Unlock their hearts." Faces began to flash through my mind. I could see people I know, love, and longed to see free from pain, addiction, and hurt.

My response was, "How do I do this?" His reply was to, "Pray and speak My Word to them. It is a double-edged sword, diving bone and marrow. It exposes the heart so that truth can get in and work on their heart." Jesus was commissioning me to unlock their hearts with His words and heart to bring truth which leads to freedom. He then spoke Matthew 5:9 to me: "Blessed are the peacemakers for they will be called sons (daughters) of God." His words resonated in my chest. He was calling me to be a peacemaker. He was sending me to the ones who lived in chaos, daily residing in pain and bondage. I was to bring *them peace. I was to reveal God's heart to them, preparing them for His truth to penetrate deep within them. Tears flooding my eyes and spilling out down my face, I stood there accepting His gifts and knowing I had been appointed that day for something beyond me.*

TAKE AWAY

That day marked me. That encounter connected me in a deeper way to the Father's heart and to my own purpose. Encounters like the one I had give us insight into who God is and who we are. It is always important to compare our encounters with God's Word. Looking back on my encounter, I truly believe that experience lined up with who I know Jesus to be. He made me feel seen, loved, and known. His gentle, generous heart gave me a ruby ring I had always wanted but never told anyone about. The ring and robe He offered signified royalty, authority, and belonging. He confirmed to my heart that day that it was not just about the ring or garment; He was showing me how He sees me – who I am. His kindness confirmed He knows what I need for myself and what I need to give out to others. The verse in Proverbs 3:15 came to mind and reminded me that God's wisdom is more precious than rubies; it alone is of worth. He was commissioning me to take His wisdom and truth to those who needed freedom because I had been given His power and authority.

The kingly garment, signet ring, and the keys of authority to His Kingdom gave me access to His righteousness, peace, and joy. Not just knowing about those things but being in possession of them gave me confidence to know I was being called to carry peace into those broken places. Encounters move us past head knowledge about a subject and give us practical experience and application that confirms the truth and revelation God desires us to know in our minds and hearts.

Because of experiences like these, I have learned that we can hear, see, feel, and know things during an encounter. During this interaction, I was able to stay in my present realm and yet experience

Him in the spirit as if He was standing in my room. He was there. His presence was there; He just wasn't standing in a solid human fleshly body. I can step out of the situation and confirm that what took place was not outside of His nature. What he showed me, said to me, and allowed me to know stayed true to who His Word says He is. I walked away from that experience confident in Him, His power, and His love. Without a doubt, I believe there is no limit to what He can do. Encounters with Him give us space to experience His goodness, His majesty, and His love in abundance in just a matter of moments.

God doesn't need our affirmation or adoration. However, as we give it, an opportunity opens up to get our gaze set on Him and step into the King's domain. Adoration leads us into the heavenly realms. Worship raises our expectations so He can raise His revelation. Our adoration and worship pull on heaven.

My prayer is that the encounters I share with you stir up a desire for you to go deeper into God's goodness. There is permission for you to use my experience as a launching point for your own. Please take this opportunity to look at the suggestions I have below (and at the end of these encounter chapters) so that you can create space for God to show up for you! He is present and willing to meet with you.

Adoration is a doorway into the heavenlies.

Questions and Reflections
...to ponder on your way to possibilities!

If adoration is a door into the heavens, then give yourself space to worship and adore Jesus, God the Father, and the Holy Spirit.

WORSHIP CREATES SPACE FOR ENCOUNTER

➤Find a quiet place, free from distractions. Play instrumental worship music or your favorite worship song.

➤Take a deep breath in and exhale out. Think about WHO God is. Tell Him what you love about that.

➤Think about the moments He showed up for you. Tell Him how thankful you are for WHO He has been for you

➤Read out loud:

➤Psalm 84:1-2 "How lovely is your dwelling place, O Lord Almighty! My soul yearns, even faints, for the courts of the Lord; my heart and my flesh cry out for the living God."

➤Lamentations 3:22-24 "Because of the Lord's great love we are not consumed, for his compassions never fail. They are new every morning, great is your faithfulness. I say to myself, 'The Lord is my portion; therefore, I will wait for him.'"

➤Worship God for His abundant love. Ask God to speak to your heart, and invite God to draw you into a deeper level of love and understanding of who He is.

➤Write or journal what you see, hear, or sense. Thank God for spending time with you.

13

ENCOUNTER OR REVELATION

THERE HAVE BEEN moments on my journey when all I longed for was a fresh word from God's heart to mine. My heart finds no greater joy than hearing or experiencing God's heart toward me. There are days when all I want is to open the Bible and have the words jump off the pages and bring encouragement to my heart. I know the verse or concept I read will bring incredible life to my soul. One word spoken at the right moment from truth and love is powerful!

There are other days when I just want to tangibly feel, hear, or see Him in an encounter. Both are vital. Both are full of life. Does one come first? I have heard it said that revelation and encounters are like revolving doors. Revelation leads you into an encounter, and an encounter back into greater revelation. For our purposes, an encounter has to do with experiencing some aspect of who God is, while a revelation is an understanding in our mind or spirit either through natural processing or divine understanding. From experience, either can come first, and one always leads you to the other (which we will see as we further explore this idea). They are two sides of the same coin.

Encounters and revelations can be received or experienced when you're alone or standing in a crowd of people. There is validity and worth to both. There is power and authenticity in either situation, and I have experienced both. No matter if I am standing quietly in the comfort of my own home or with others, I appreciate it when God shows up. I would never want to deny Him access to my heart.

There are times when I feel one would be timelier for me. For instance, when my heart is in a place where it can't handle words or process understanding because the week has been full and I am overloaded. In that place, a good Father knows that reading words or processing revelation won't be as refreshing as an encounter. God uses those moments to show up on a heart level in *experience*. He allows me to sense and feel because my receptors are more open for that in those times.

Sometimes we need an encounter before revelation fully comes. There are moments when our filter will not allow us to fully understand who God is unless we meet Him face to face. Those times are more transformative or meaningful to our hearts and minds if we are invited to walk through and experience it rather than just being given information or engaging in conversation. God designed us to be experiential beings. Sometimes we learn better by doing. From the action we acquire the understanding.

Having an encounter can also be beneficial during moments when our hearts are too tired, worn, or wounded and we need to experience His presence as restorative and healing like a gentle massage for sore muscles. As stated before, one leads to the other. The revelation is birthed out of the encounter. He doesn't just show up so we can see and feel His love, although that is a huge part of it. He wants us to know about His love so we can communicate it to others. This gives them the opportunity to learn about it and experience it also.

Revelation is sometimes needed before the encounter. Our emotions and senses are not always awake enough or ready for the actual experience. That is when our good Father comes gently speaking our language and revealing information and knowledge to us first. He knows when we need to know how a car works, why we press the long skinny pedal, and how important the one in the middle is for stopping! He knows we need to know which side of the road to drive on and what the signal lights are. Then, He hands us keys to the car and gets in to ride with us.

There are moments when we must first have a revelation or understanding before we can experience the weight and depth of what He wants to show us. There are times before anything else happens when we need a revelation of who we are or who God is. There is revelation and knowledge that helps prepare us for what we will encounter. The understanding of what God has done, the sin He bore, the price He paid, and the beating He took on our behalf all lead us into an encounter with His goodness, and ultimately a time of thanksgiving and worship! Our head and heart are connected. They speak to each other and rely upon each other for clarification and guidance. His peace and power come on a tangible level.

I am not saying one is better than the other. Both are THE WORD. We can read the words of Jesus on a page and have revelation lead us into encountering who He is. Reading His words are just as powerful as encountering the Word in flesh, Jesus. His spoken words and His nature, who He is, brings life and refreshing to our souls. Experiencing who He is brings further revelation of who He is. Revelation and encounter are both vital. Ultimately, God knows which one we need first. This is exactly what I have experienced, like I did one evening when I was worshiping with friends under the stars.

MY ENCOUNTER AT THE KING'S TABLE

As I stood in an atmosphere of praise, my heart honed in on the greatness of my God. Standing there, under the night sky, listening to the voices and instruments create such beautiful melodies, my heart postured itself for an encounter. I set my gaze on a great, big God. My heart leaned into His strength. Any worry or burden paled in comparison to His majestic nature. The air around me, cool and fresh, gave space for me to ponder His worth and holiness. Understanding filled my heart and ached because His goodness, truth, and love became so real and tangible. I longed for more of Him. My heart turned from understanding and revelation into adoration. From that place, I fell to my knees in awe of His kindness, goodness, and affection toward me. In that space of worship, where my knees almost melted into the cold concrete, I was apprehended by His love. Under the stars, my heart chose to surrender.

At that moment, my mind began playing out a version of what was happening there in our corporate worship gathering. In the natural (this natural realm), people were gathered, standing, sitting, and kneeling in worship. If I had opened my eyes, I would have seen hands extended out and up to the heavens, some lifted high in adoration and others low in surrender. In the natural, voices sang out thanksgiving and praise to a King seated on the throne. That was physical, but my heart yearned for what I could see (not in the physical) in the realm just past the thin unseen curtain that hangs between this world and the spiritual realm. My heart yearned to go into the scene being played out in my mind.

As my mind refocused from what was taking place around me to what was happening outside of the earthly surroundings, I began to see a large wooden table. This strong table, made of rugged wood, had carvings on the side and legs. There it stood, naked before us in the throne room...waiting. In the imagination of my mind, with my eyes closed off to the people standing around me, I began to see hands reach out and place dishes on the table. One set of hands placed a platter of plain bread. Another pair of hands placed a goblet of wine, and still another bowl of delicious grapes. The table was being set for the King.

At that moment, encounter and understanding were having a dance. I began to realize that naturally our worship and praise had put us in a position to bring our sacrifice to the King. Our sacrifice of praise, songs pouring from our lips and hearts devoted to worship, set the table and provided a beautiful feast fit for the King. Each life brought what they could bring. The humble heart who felt they had nothing extravagant to bring brought their life – a simple loaf of bread. A life hard pressed on every side and weighed down by affliction and worry brought a glass of the most precious and pressed fruit which became wine. The excited heart that had tasted and seen God's goodness brought the overflow of His kindness and presented the juiciest, most deliciously large grapes. From the broken to the blessed, each life brought their worship and set the table for the King.

In that moment of beauty, my heart found peace and joy. This incredible table had been set for the King. The expectation was heightened as the King sat viewing the incredible presentation and sacrifices that had been brought. He stood at the front of the table with such joy at the feast before Him. My heart was pounding, excited to see what He would say about the gifts we brought. That is when He turned to each person who brought their sacrifice of praise and said, "Eat at the table, for I have prepared it for you in the sight of your enemies."

TAKE AWAY

Can we just pause for a moment? I can honestly say my heart was not ready for that encounter. Even now, I can hardly write these words; tears are spilling down my cheeks. This incredible encounter that danced between experience and understanding had me prepared to rejoice that we had brought our worship to God, each one of us coming with what we had to offer. But it became so much deeper. That picture is rich in so many ways and touches on some incredible truths which will hit you at your core. Let's talk about it and start with the end and work backwards. I know some of you just flinched. You might be saying, "My brain can't work backwards." Trust me, it's a key truth that will make the rest of the encounter make sense. Here is the truth: the sacrifice wasn't just meant for the King.

In that encounter, God reveals a key aspect about worship. It isn't just about the one who is giving adoration or bowing in surrender. Nor is it only about the one receiving the worship and being surrendered to. It is about the relationship between the two. It is about the motive, the act, and the outcome! Sometimes you have to see the end from the beginning, and sometimes you realize it's so interwoven it might be hard to separate them. Here, the last phrase is the start of it all, *"Eat at the table, for I have prepared it for you in the sight of your enemies."* We are invited to eat at a table that has been set for us, though we were the ones bringing the offerings.

Did you hear the Father? God cannot put away His Father's heart, and though we heard it spoken by the King who sits high above it all, those words also came from a Father who looks at His children and says, "Thank you for your offering. This feast is for you." Wait, did you catch that? It was set for us! We had brought our sacrifice as a gift to set the table for Him, right? We offered our praise which gave this gift to our God and King. Yet in that moment of surrender, the King of it all who is also a good Father now turns the gift back on His children.

The King's table is being offered to us with the ability to eat this feast. His goodness gives us back everything we brought in surrender to Him. He is not a Father in the habit of keeping or withholding goodness. He is not selfish to keep for Himself that which rightfully belongs to Him. Instead, He chooses to feast with us! In the middle of that moment, my tears of gratitude could not be contained, and my heart was full as I stood in worship and feasted with my King.

The adoration and the surrender we partnered with that night set the table for the King to feast. This encounter teaches us how our surrender and worship bring sacrifices to the rough wooden altar. The carved side and legs of that table reflect the scarred side, feet, and hands of Jesus the Savior who hung on the cross for you and me. The sacrifices we bring, our lives, are placed on the table. This brings to mind a picture of how we abide in Christ. It was accepted as an offering of worship, and then it was given back to the giver. Just as it was for me, this is an invitation for you to join the King in celebration. Encounters lead us to revelation, which leads us back into greater encounters. It is a beautifully wonderful circle of true and abundant life.

~

I appreciate it when God shows up. I would never want to deny Him access to my heart.

Questions and Reflections
...to ponder on your way to Possibilities!

If surrender allows us to give our lives and then receive goodness from Him, what areas of your life need to be surrendered?

SURRENDER CREATES SPACE FOR ENCOUNTER

➤Quiet your heart. Pray out loud and tell God you want to surrender your life fully to Him.

➤Ask God if there is any lie you are believing that has kept you from receiving His goodness.

➤If a situation comes to mind, pray out loud saying, "God, I break off the power of this lie I have been believing. I diminish its power over me because of the sacrifice You made for me on the cross and the freedom You bought for me."

➤Ask Him for the truth that He wants you to believe.

➤If a statement or verse comes to mind, pray out loud saying, "God, I choose to partner with Your truth for me which says (fill in the blank)."

➤Thank Him for the truth and declare, "I am free from (_____) because of the blood of Jesus, and I will walk in (_____) because He has secured that truth for me."

➤Worship and thank God for His freedom.

➤Ask God to speak to your heart. Invite God to draw you into a deeper understanding of who He is.

➤Write or journal what you see, hear, or sense. Thank God for the way He is meeting you personally.

14

PUSHING US OUT OF OUR BOXES

When I was a young girl, part of me wanted to pursue gymnastics or dance. It wasn't my career goal, but there was something beautiful and freeing about the act. Maybe every girl has a dream about the ballerina shoes and what they will magically do for her when she slips them on. When I took gymnastics lessons, I loved the aspects of the floor routine or beam that involved grace and fluidity of movement. Somewhere along my journey, I stopped dancing and became self-conscious of movement. Every once in a while, my inner dancer would come out, maybe at a wedding, and I would pretend for a while.

When my husband and I were courting after college, a group of us ladies thought it would be fun to learn different styles of dance. We gathered our men and headed off to the studio to learn different styles. Some of the guys weren't as thrilled with the idea, but they must have realized they could hold our hands and get pretty close, so they were good sports. One of the first things the instructor did was have us learn the box step. With our feet, we followed an imaginary square around the floor, making a complete box after all the steps were taken. From that structure, we then were able to learn more advanced patterns that gave us freedom outside the box.

Of all the styles we learned, my favorite was swing. The syncopation, rhythm, kicks, and stunts involved made dancing really fun. We were not limited to a simple, boring box pattern around the floor. There was excitement and adventure involved in all of that, unless you ask my then boyfriend who is now my husband. It frustrated him so much. Although none of the dance styles were his favorite, the safety of the box pattern was more his speed. The structure, predictability, and ease gave him comfort.

There is something comforting about knowing what comes next. The predictability and simplicity of a box can help avoid anxiety and even missteps. However, what I learned during our short season of dance is that the exhilaration, fun, and joy came when we got pushed out of our box steps and embraced a style with more freedom.

The same is true in our spiritual journey. There is something necessary about knowing the basics and becoming comfortable with the simple structure of the box so we can build upon it. But like dance, we must realize there comes a time when even those who do a formal genre of dance open up their box and embrace the freedom that happens beyond its borders.

When we are in pursuit of encountering God's presence, allowing His Spirit to come and meet us, there will be stay-in-the-box moments as well as moments we are asked to step out into freedom. Encounters are never one sided nor are they formula based. Encounters are meetings that stir new levels of relationship. They are about exchanging our hearts with God's in an experience that doesn't look the same every time. We can't limit encounters to a method or particular picture. They will look different for every individual. What will not change, is the nature of God that will be reflected during the encounter. He is the same yesterday, today, and forever. Even so, it doesn't mean the way we experience Him will be the same as our neighbor or even the same from one day to the next. We can't predict, but we can prepare and make ourselves aware of His nudging and invitations into the "more" He longs to show us! That is exactly what I did as I stood alone in my living room one night.

MY ENCOUNTER WITH FREEDOM

My heart was weighed down with concerns. So, in the stillness of my living room with worship music playing softly, I stood in the darkness and just breathed. Inhale. Exhale. I listened to every note, as it chipped away at the heaviness that felt like boulders on my shoulders. My spirit stirred in me, and though my flesh was tired, weary, and worn, something in me cried out for freedom. Inhale. Exhale. The burden felt a little lighter.

In the darkness, free from any spectators, I stood. Then, I had a thought – a subtle prompting deep inside. The thought from that familiar voice, which I had learned was my gracious Heavenly Father, was gently encouraging me to step out of the box of comfort. He was gently giving me permission to be me. He was reminding me the place I was longing for could only be entered into like a child. As I stood in the stillness of the room, a melody filled my head and heart. I began to move. With my feet pointed and my arms extended, I danced like a child. With every move, my arms and legs pushed the confines of the imaginary box I was stuck in. As I did, my heart became joyful, giddy, and I danced alone in that room...freer than I had felt in a long time.

This act of worship, unpolished and playful, had unlocked my heart. This return to childlikeness had broken me free of the weights and concerns I felt as a wife and mother. This playfulness with my Father, in the quiet places of my worship time, had brought a new freedom and joy I had been longing for. And after I had danced and worshiped, I once again stood. Inhale. Exhale. There was a new freedom. The burden had been lifted.

Without hearing words, my spirit sensed there was another part to this encounter. I just knew deep inside that there was an exchange to take place. In the stillness of the dark room, I stood with my hands outstretched and cupped in front of me ready to receive a gift. I stood in surrender, waiting in expectation, with tears spilling down my cheeks. Inhale. Exhale. My hands started to feel like something was being poured into them.

In my imagination, with my eyes closed, I could see a picture of a bottle tipping out over my hands. A substance was being poured into my hands, and I could tangibly feel them getting heavier. My cupped hands were becoming full of what felt like oil; I could feel it running down the sides of my hands and in between my fingers. Each hand was overflowing with oil, while tears streamed down my face, spilling onto my hands, mixing with the oil. With it came such gratitude, joy, and peace.

I don't know how long I stood there. I didn't want to move. The presence of God was so tangible, literally tangible like oil. His love, joy, and peace was felt. It circled all around me and washed over me. I stood there for as long as I could. Inhale. Exhale. I stayed in the presence.

TAKE AWAY

God never shows up as you expect. He always comes in ways which exceed our imagination. He knows what we need and when we need it. He knows how far out of the box He can show up so we still feel safe and yet drawn into more. God loves to bring us into more love, more hope, more refreshing. His abundance and invitation to more is about awareness. It is about understanding and experiencing His goodness and allowing it to transform us inside and out. He is a God of more.

That day, I felt weighed down. I was carrying burdens that needed to be dropped. The stirring in my heart was to get free. The way I did it was by stepping out of my adult mindset and allowing my heart to dance like a child full of freedom. I didn't walk into the room that night with an expectation to dance. Instead, I surrendered my heart as I stood, worshiped, and listened to the nudges of the Holy Spirit. God knew my body needed to move first, and then my heart and head would catch up. His gentle nudge to press in, lean forward, and take the first step is what drew me into the encounter. Choosing to dance before the Lord with no self-reservation was not new, just necessary. Obedience woke up my senses and gave me an opportunity to break off the weight and burdens I was carrying. It left me awake, aware, and ready for Him to fill my cup to overflow.

I imagine King David experienced a similar feeling as he danced with wild abandonment. The people were shouting, the trumpets blew with zeal, and this king dancing in his tunic didn't care about how he looked or what others thought. His excitement to have God's presence near was all he cared about. All of his energy was focused on praising a God who deserved his praise. His wild worship came from a heart that was grateful to be chosen and loved by God.

Thankfulness and necessity were motivations for his excitement. David had experienced God's presence and the anointing that comes with choosing. Now, he was chosen to be king; the prophet anointed him with oil. This act set him apart to give him purpose and honor by, "Anointing [his] head with oil [causing his cup to] overflow with blessings" (Psalm 23:5 NLT). This act of smearing or rubbing oil on someone was equivalent to crowning them as royalty and affirmed their assignment and authority. David knew he was chosen and appointed. He knew that pouring out oil was a sign of God's Spirit, power, and provision.

Just like he did for me that night, God can take your burdens, giving you freedom in their place. Through encounters, maybe even dance, you can step into green pastures and allow Him to restore your soul. Stepping out of your comfort, into obedience, will let His Spirit nudge you down good paths, journeying closer to His heart and toward freedom. Your heart will find ease and your fear will disappear because you will give space to become like a child who feels protected, safe, and loved by a good Father.

I hear some of you saying, "I didn't feel protected or safe as a child." Here is where you get to step out of the box you were forced to live in as a child. Now is the opportunity to disempower those old mindsets. Obedience draws you into new levels of freedom, and after you push past your insecurity and uncomfortability, you will see more of who you are and who God is.

Just like me, you will get to see a side of the good Father that maybe you have never known. After I had worshiped, danced, laughed, and cried, I stood. I was overwhelmed with His goodness, and I knew I had the opportunity to breathe in His comfort and refreshing while exhaling my burdens. So can you. God is waiting for you to step into moments of refreshing. He desires you to know the permission you have; inhale His peace and exhale the cares. He wants you to stand loved and chosen, covered by His blessings, power, and Spirit. He longs to affirm you belong and have authority. His Spirit is abundant and ready to anoint you with fragrant oil, filling your cup to overflowing as you step out of your box into His *more*.

There will be stay-in-the-box moments as well as moments we are asked to step out into freedom.

Questions and Reflections
...to ponder on your way to possibilities!

If you are carrying burdens too heavy to carry or holding onto mindsets full of limitations, then releasing them will enlarge your heart and mind for greater refreshment.

RELEASING CREATES SPACE FOR ENCOUNTER

➤ Quiet your body; become still. Imagine the burden you have been carrying (or the old mindset that needs to be renewed).

➤ Breathe in and exhale. Declare out loud that you want to release the burden and hand it over to God. Imagine handing it to Him or setting it at the foot of the cross.

➤ Pray out loud and say, "God, I give You my (fill in the blank). I do not want to carry more than You have asked me to."

➤ Ask Him if there is ANY LIE you believed about His goodness or your burden. If a statement or lie comes to mind, pray out loud saying, "God, I break off the lie that _____."

➤ Ask Him for the truth that *He wants* you to believe. If a statement or verse comes to mind, pray out loud saying, "God, I choose to partner with Your truth for me which says _____."

➤ Thank God for **knowing what you need.** Thank Him for times of **refreshing and renewal.**

➤ Ask God to speak to your heart and reveal something about His Fatherhood that you need to understand or experience. Invite God to draw you into a deeper relationship with His refreshing peace.

➤ Write or journal what you see, hear, or sense. Thank God for **being present for you.**

15

UNEXPECTED ENCOUNTERS

Encountering the heart of the Father is vital and should be a priority. That being said, not every revelation or encounter is expected. There is a posturing and hunger that draws Jesus close – a desire to which He always responds to. However, we can't force an encounter. What I mean is that sometimes God surprises us and steps into our space suddenly or in unexpected ways. (We looked at the unexpected a little in chapter 12.) We don't have to have the perfect atmosphere for Jesus to show up. He meets us where we are. He sees our hearts; He knows our deepest needs. There is no situation, question, or feeling that He doesn't already have the solution to.

As a busy mom of three toddlers, I tried to take advantage of rare quiet moments (while my kids were down for their naps) to recharge. Some days that meant a physical nap, but most of the time I really just wanted to get a spiritual supercharge from a sermon or a word spoken directly to my heart. Early in motherhood, I made it a practice to pray and listen to sermons while folding laundry, washing dishes, or even eating lunch in the quiet of my room. Don't judge, but I remember putting the cassette tape into the tape player to do this.

Yes, I have lived through tapes and CD's before streaming or podcasts.

During one of those times, I was listening to a well-respected preacher who came annually to our church. He had been a missionary for many years, and I loved listening to him (partly because he had this incredible British accent) because he was full of faith and told stories that always left me excited about what the Holy Spirit could do.

SUDDEN WIND

During his message, he began to talk about how BIG Jesus is. The verses he used and the stories he told, always pointed back to God's goodness and how the Holy Spirit is able to do more than we can even fathom. This particular day, I was sitting in my room eating lunch at my desk. The words he spoke came from his heart straight into my room. I could hear his voice, his heart, but I could also hear people from the audience in the background. During his message, the faint sound of laughter blew through the background. Slowly, you could hear the laughter gently spread like a breeze through the room. As I was listening, I could actually hear the wind and laughter which started quietly from someplace in the crowd. It didn't erupt violently, but it did increase, and as it got closer to his microphone, there was an intensity.

Then, mid-bite, without planning it, I chuckled at the sound of the joy that had become more explosive on the recording of his message. Sitting at my desk, I felt the Holy Spirit wash over me like a wave. I could tangibly feel His presence – love, joy, and peace. I not only sensed it in the room, like He was standing next to me, but I felt it bubbling up from within me. I was overwhelmed by the intensity and power of the Holy Spirit, and I toggled between chuckles and tears. Before I could decide, I began weeping, overcome by the tangible love of a good Father. A second before this, I had taken a bite of my sandwich, and a moment later I almost spit it all out as the weeping turned into more intense sobs which came uncontrollably.

Without thinking, I stood up, crumbs falling off my lap, and raised my hands in surrender. Then, the presence grew stronger; the only response that seemed appropriate was to lay down flat on my belly on the floor of my room. As I did, the presence grew even stronger and the weight of the Holy Spirit rested on me in a more powerful way, causing me to tremble. It wasn't trembling out of fear or sorrow. The intensity of God's tangible presence had brought with it an electricity that pulsed through my body. Due to the weightiness of His presence, I stayed on the floor, just letting the wind of the Spirit, the majestic glory, and the intense power of God wash over me. It was as if the wind kept blowing from the direction of the tape player. It blew out over me, over the room, and I laid in His presence.

TAKE AWAY

During this encounter I felt as if I was being refreshed. My heart's cry, before that moment even occurred, was to know and experience more of His presence. He showed up suddenly in this moment to answer my cry and draw me closer. In that place of peace, delight, and surrender, my inner being just cried out for more. It was a hunger to know and encounter God in His fullness. That day on my lunch break, my need for food became a spiritual picture of me finding a refueling by power. HE became my source and the One who filled me.

Jesus taught that we are happy if we hunger or crave the things He values. Those who have an appetite for the right things (Kingdom things) will be full of joy and see blessings. I love how The Passion Translation says it: "How enriched you are when you crave righteousness! For you will be satisfied" (Matthew 5:6 TPT). That encounter left me enriched and satisfied. I knew deep down I craved more of Him. I had made that confession plenty of times before that day, but I didn't pick the moment when He answered. Instead, my heart responded to what He had begun with the group of people who sat in that recorded meeting years before I ever listened to that cassette tape. God's Spirit moved in their room that day, and because His presence is alive outside of our world's limitations, He was not confined to time or space. He responded to their hunger then and to my hunger now.

God loves to show up and lead us into an encounter during our normal daily life. Even in the regular activities of laundry, cleaning, and eating, He knows our hearts cry and wants us to encounter Him. He walks alongside us on our journey through this life and wants us to encounter righteousness, peace, and joy – all His Kingdom things. He knows how to gently speak to our heart, show us His goodness, prove just how BIG He is, and reveal He is right there with us.

It reminds me of one of the most interesting stories about Jesus. After Jesus was brutally beaten, crucified, and buried, His disciples were told His body was not in the tomb. Angels had appeared to the women, and the entire town was talking about these events. Two of the disciples are on their way out of Jerusalem, distraught, confused, and even disappointed. As they walked, they processed the events. Along the way, a man traveling by foot joins them on their journey. In the middle of their mess, the real-life processing moments, someone walks into their story. The man joins their daily activity and conversation, and then they spend their moments processing their disappointment and confusion.

It was not until the end of their day, when they stopped for dinner, that everything started to make sense. This man they invited to stay for dinner took the bread from the middle of the dinner table, spoke words of blessing, and then handed it out to the group. "All at once their eyes were opened and they realized he was Jesus! Then suddenly, in a flash, Jesus vanished before their eyes! Stunned, they looked at each other and said, 'Why didn't we recognize him? Didn't our hearts burn with the flames of holy passion while we walked beside him?'" (Luke 24:30 TPT).

Just like the disciples that day, we can go about our daily activities and miss the truth being spoken to our heart about the risen Savior. We can walk our journey and even entertain conversations about or with Jesus. However, distraction, disappointment, and confusion can keep us from wholeness. Until we stop, show hunger (break bread), and have our eyes opened in revelation to who God is for us, we will miss the power of a mighty God who is walking right beside us.

That day during my lunch, mid bite, I had a revelation of Jesus and His incredible love for me. The joy and peace I felt stirred every emotion. Truth burned so deep in me, my heart was on fire, and I couldn't help but lay down in surrender because of the overwhelming love coursing through my body like electricity. The power I experienced wasn't just raw energy, it was His resurrection power that brought refreshing to my tired and hungry heart. I had my eyes opened to how BIG Jesus is and how much He loves me. My response matched the passion I felt burning inside.

Jesus loves to step into our lives and bring revelation, but did you notice that He didn't stay there with the disciples? His presence and revelation were an invitation for them to keep pursuing more. The burning we feel in our chest when we hear about God's goodness and truth is an invitation for more. The burning is confirmation of the gift He left for us. He walked this earth, but once He completed his assignment—redemption for humanity—He left this earth. He didn't just leave us alone; He left His Holy Spirit for us. Jesus gives us what we need for the rest of the journey.

His presence is alive outside of our world's limitations
...not confined to time or space.

Questions and Reflections
…to ponder on your way to possibilities!

If God wants to show up in your everyday activities, invite Him into those places.

AWARENESS CREATES SPACE FOR ENCOUNTER

➤ While doing the dishes, laundry, or driving, allow yourself permission to become aware of what God is doing. Verbalize that you will respond to His invitation into revelation or encounter when you realize He is there working.

➤ Tell God He can show up anytime. Give Him the opportunity to speak.

➤ Put on a sermon or podcast that is centered around God's truths.

➤ Listen for the one thing that jumps out at you and meets your heart where it is.

➤ Pray out loud and say, "God, I want You to meet me in that place"

➤ Do what he tells you to do!

➤ If a verse comes to mind, stop what you are doing and look it up.

➤ If a song comes to mind, sing it or stream it.

➤ If a person comes to mind, pray for them and ask God to give you encouragement to share with them.

➤ Invite God to draw you into a deeper relationship with His heart.

➤ Write or journal what you see, hear, or sense. Thank God for **showing up in your everyday life.**

16

INVITATION INTO ENCOUNTER

THE ENVELOPE ARRIVED; the crisp white canvas had my name written on it in beautiful calligraphy. I gently turned it over and tried to open it without tearing the precious contents. Nestled inside was the invitation I had been waiting for. Picked out with intent, carefully selected to showcase the experience we would have, it was beautifully written as a summons inviting us into their joy.

Invitations are full of excitement. Invitations tell us there is value to our relationship, and we have been chosen to join others in celebration. They are about an experience, not just words printed on a paper, and based on relationship. That invitation gives us access because we are more than familiar —— we are known and chosen.

Like the invitation the mail carrier leaves in our mailbox, we are given both tangible and inner longings that are an invitation into more. I grew up in a family that understood the importance of having a personal relationship with God the Father, Jesus, and Holy Spirit. I was taught how to give space to encounter an incredible God. Even as a young girl, I knew I could talk to God and He would faithfully speak back. I understood there was permission to know Him personally through His Word, His voice, dreams, and visions. My parents modeled relationships, worship, and encountering the Holy Spirit as a person who interacts with us today!

INVITED INTO INTIMACY

We are called into relationship. As we navigate what it looks like to interact in relationship with an unseen God, we can learn the importance of *being*. With human interaction with those we love, we understand we don't want to miss any opportunities to be with them. The same is true with our relationship with a good Heavenly Father. I don't want to miss a chance to experience and stay in His presence. Being with Him is like the picture of marinating ourselves in His goodness. We know the busy life we are used to, and unfortunately we often disregard this crucial step of being with Him. We have looked at remaining and abiding. This is directly connected. *Being* or allowing space for us to just sit with an open heart is vital.

As physical and spiritual beings, our lives reside here on earth, but our identity is attached to eternity. Eternity is set in our hearts because we are created in His image. He is eternal. The Bible gives us a list of things He is. He is *love*. He is *the way*. He is *truth*, and like He says, "I AM." When He calls us into greater identity, He calls us into who He is. As He *is,* so are we to *be*.

Intimacy is about *being*. Reflecting on this, my mind immediately goes to the verse in Psalm 46:10 which says, "Stop striving and know that I am God" (NASB). Two words from that powerfully short verse jump out to me: s*triving* and *know*. First, we see that striving doesn't produce relationship. We don't work for intimacy; we experience it. By saying this, I am not saying relationships aren't work. What I am saying is that intimacy comes from being, sitting, staying in presence. The meaning behind the word *know* has to do with experiencing – not having head knowledge about but intimate understanding. Spending time being present and intentional is part of building relationships. Staying in God's presence fosters intimacy with the Holy Spirit. That is the goal of the encounter.

ENCOUNTERS ARE ABOUT MORE

Throughout my years of encountering God in different ways, I have wavered between being full and hungry for more. Long ago, my heart said I will take whatever God will allow me to have. I say that tongue in cheek, because I believe God does not withhold anything good from His children. He desires to show up for us just as much as we desire to see Him. As we are faithful to steward the time we set aside, He is faithful to encounter us and to give us more. This could mean setting aside time to listen to Holy Spirit and record His words. Stewarding encounters could look like sharing the revelation we got with someone to encourage their heart. Every day we have the opportunity to go deeper and deeper and experience the *more* in Him.

Creating space for greater intimacy can lead us into throne-room encounters. This requires us to carve out opportunities to sit with Him; no striving. Sitting in stillness or silence allows our mind and heart to disconnect from performance or work. We open up space to receive instead of just pouring out, which provides a way to refuel our empty tank. In this open space, we tune our ears to the sound-waves of heaven. It is a time of replenishing instead of depletion. It is a time of listening and hearing – a crucial practice when we have deep questions or concerns weighing on our hearts.

Sitting in stillness with Scripture can be an incredible way to be present with God. He is the living and active part of the words penned on paper, and He will interact with us as we meditate on who He is and what He has done. Often, an encounter can come from the things God is actively working in us, even as we go about our day. When we take a minute to stop, He brings something to mind and meets us in those words, places, and spaces. I have had encounters take place during a dream or as I am waking up. There have been moments I woke up from a deep sleep, and in my awake state, I asked God why I was woken up. He showed me why as He met me in that place of inquiry. Whether asleep or awake, God longs to draw us to Himself and address our deepest concerns and longings.

As we interact and encounter Jesus, we can ask God to show us principles in the Bible that match what we have experienced. Because He is faithful and constant, His nature doesn't change, and who He is for us and to us can also be seen as we look through Scripture. One day, I read a different translation of a verse I had read many times before. When I read it, God brought a previous encounter back to my mind and gave me greater understanding about it. The Passion Translations version of Psalm 18:1-2 says, "I love you, Yahweh, and I'm bonded to you, my strength! Yahweh, you're the bedrock beneath my feet, my faith-fortress, my wonderful deliverer, my God, my rock of rescue where none can reach me. You're the shield around me, the mighty power that saves me, and my high place." God has shown up as the bedrock beneath my feet, and from that deep place of encounter, I experienced a greater understanding of being bonded to Him. His words were and are an invitation for me to stand on Him and then fall to my face, pressing into Him as I rest in knowing we are bonded.

HALLWAY OF STONE

There I stood, looking around to see where I was. I strained to see what was around me, but couldn't because it was pitch black. The only thing I knew was I was in a narrow hallway standing on a slab of rock. I could feel the rigidness of the rock below me. My feet could tell it wasn't a smooth concrete floor.

My eyes began to adjust, and faintly I could see rows of closed doors on either side of the hallway. As I stood there wondering about them, I sensed a caution to stop. I stopped. I waited. My spirit told me not to forge ahead and open any doors. My spirit said, pause. Just be. In the waiting, I knew I wasn't supposed to move forward without God's direction. My heart cried out for a light to come show me the way. My spirit cried out, asking God to show me where to go.

No sooner had my thoughts inquired of Him, then suddenly a footprint was illuminated on the floor. It glowed with brilliance in the silent darkness. With control, I stepped onto the footprint, but aside from that one print, darkness remained around me.

I waited. Again, my heart cried out, "God what should I do next?" I didn't feel fear. I wasn't alone. I was standing on an illuminated print of His making. He was with me. I was standing in stillness, then another footprint appeared. It radiantly lit up another step, and so I moved forward one step, standing on His footprint.

This same pattern continued for a few minutes, and then all of a sudden, the illumination stopped. The air remained silent, dark, and nothing but wondering was present. What is going on? Has my journey ended? Do I just stay in the middle of the hallway with no outlet? There are only closed doors around me. What is my next move?

I wondered. I waited. I was.

Soon after, I could feel the inside of me vibrate. My eyes were being drawn to the cold, rugged rock beneath my feet. It was as if a magnet drew my eyes, then the very core of me down towards the floor. So, I bent down. I kneeled. The lower I got, the clearer the image was below me. As I bent down, I could see His face in the rock beneath me. He was present. His eyes beckoned me.

Everything in me felt compelled to get down, to go low. So, I laid myself prostrate on the hard ground. I thought, "I am not kneeling down, I am getting as close to His face as I can." I pressed my face against His. My eyes were aligned with His. My mouth covered the outline of His mouth, and I laid there as close to Him as I could.

Laying there, I waited. He then came rushing in, pouring like liquid love into every cell of my being. As I laid there, He poured Himself into me. He filled me up so full with His glory. I felt full of His love, overwhelmed by His compassion, truth, light, and life. There I stayed...so full. In fact, I felt so full that in my dream I was paralyzed. I could not move.

And then I woke up. I was no longer in a dream state. I was in my room, on my bed, and yet I couldn't move. No longer on a slab floor, my eyes looked around as if they were the only thing that could move. Just as it had been in the dream, my body was heavy and I felt *paralyzed. But now fully awake, the feeling remained. I was stiff and weighed down by what could only be described as His glory. I was saturated with love, truth, and life. He had deposited himself into me. By His Spirit, He had filled me with parts of Himself into my core. I was still, heavy, and full of peace.*

For quite a while it was like this; I don't know how many minutes went by. I was content and just resting in the incredible fullness I felt. I didn't want to move. I laid there, tears in my eyes, thankful for the encounter that took me from a place of uncertainty and darkness to a place of fullness in His light and love.

TAKE AWAY

God draws us to Himself. There is a desire in our hearts to know, with an intimate experience, who God is. We don't just want to know *about* Him. Being with Him is like being surrounded by liquid love. His love and goodness seep into every crack and crevice of our lives so we feel refreshed. We don't just hear about it; He SHOWS up for us. HE shows us Himself. We don't just read words on a page or hear stories about who He is. Because He *is* peace and *is* love, we can tangibly experience those things in our hearts, mind, and body.

When our emotions or situations feel out of control, we can press our face into His and feel the solid stone of who He is stabilizing us from the inside. There is a physical act of getting low like I exhibit in some of my encounters. My physical being responded by kneeling, bowing, or laying on the ground as an act of submission and humility. The physical can come as a response to internal humility and hunger, or it can be an act that then aligns our body, mind, and spirit to this idea of going low. Whether you get low in your heart or with your body, the posture leads us deeper. We can do this because there is safety and security in His presence. He is a strong foundation; He is the rock on whom we can stand or fall.

In a matter of moments, that dream took me on a journey like the one we have been talking about. I realized I had passed through the red-light moments asking questions, gathering insight, and waiting for his direction. Those moments were followed by an attitude choice. I chose to be expectant, thankful, and joyful that He was present. In that place, I found the door of intimacy open up.

You may be able to relate to moments when doors open in places we least expect. Sometimes clear direction comes, directing us to keep walking the way we have been. However, sometimes the answer comes to us in a different way. We think God will open the door just off the hallway, but other times He presents us with an encounter before we move forward. This door into intimacy might be right under our feet, not appearing like a door at all.

Intimacy, direction, and ultimately destination comes when we get low and put our face next to His face. In that place of humility and vulnerability, we press into Him. God responds by filling us up. As we go deeper into intimacy, we realize we have a higher perspective and get positioned to go further in pursuit of who God is and who He created us to be. Mindsets shift, understanding develops, and encounters introduce us to hunger.

You might be wondering, "How can we just sit and be with someone we can't see, touch, or audibly hear?" It takes intentional practice and pursuit. By consistent and intentional *being,* we develop a set of skills that comes from everything we have been discussing through the pages of this book: patience, faith, attitude, altitude, and intentionality to encounter Him in our everyday life. The skills we acquire in action must be applied to *being*, and the insight you find in the *being* will empower you for the *doing.*

My prayer is that the encounters I have shared with you have lit a fire inside your soul to desire regular encounters with the Father, Jesus, and Holy Spirit. They want to meet you. They long to enter your situations, your questions, and your invitations. As you read how I experienced encounters, there is permission for you to go after greater intimacy with a loving God who wants you to know His heart.

Join in His conversation. Be aware of His voice while reading his

Word, listening in stillness, or by opening your imagination to see. The goal is to have a relationship with Him. We can engage with His truth and revelations of His promises for our destiny. When we press into Him, encounters are some of the highlights along the way. I long for you to set aside time and space to enter these significant moments. They are crucial to satisfy the craving of your soul.

Allow yourself time before moving on. Don't miss this opportunity for an encounter. God wants to meet with you. He longs to show you more of Himself and connect His heart to yours, meeting your deepest need. He can be the bedrock you need in this turbulent world, and He can provide the strength and direction you desire as you draw close to Him in intimacy.

~

Intimacy is about being, sitting,
and staying in His presence.

Questions and Reflections
...to ponder on your way to possibilities!

If God is attracted to humility and vulnerability, how can you position your face next to His?

INTIMACY CREATES SPACE FOR ENCOUNTER

➤ Spend time in God's Word. His words are life and teach us about who He is. Start by reading Ephesians 1:1-14.

➤ Ask the Holy Spirit to make those words come alive.

➤ Write down the words or verses that jump off the page to you.

➤ Pray and ask Him to speak directly to your heart about that word or verse.

➤ Write down what you sense, hear, or imagine Him saying.

➤ Press in closer. Ask Him for the deeper truth in those words. What truth can be found if you dig beyond the initial thoughts? Write them down.

➤ Declare those truths. Whatever He speaks, begin to declare:

> *I am _____.*
> *God, you are_____.*
> *God you will _____.*

➤ Write or journal what you see, hear, or sense. Thank God for ***drawing closer***.

Part four

HUNGER

17

APPETITE

All eyes were on the hugely pregnant five-foot-tall woman, fighting to pull herself four feet up in the air into a lifted truck. It had become a daily occurrence. I was a very pregnant mother of twins. If you asked me, I would tell you that I felt as wide as I was tall. My belly jetted out in front of me for days. I was so thankful for those precious little ones growing, but I was uncomfortable with how much I was growing too!

When I arrived at the ice cream shop for the third day in a row, I thought I was going to be banned from the place. It wasn't just that a very pregnant lady was coming in for another shake, it was that I arrived in my husband's lifted truck that required a crane to successfully lift me in and out. I don't remember why I was driving his truck; I just remember the extreme desire for ice cream.

You must know, that the craving wasn't mine. I was there to get ice cream for my husband. I promise. Yes, I was pregnant and at times had a craving, but the reality of this moment was that my husband's jaw was wired shut, and I was feeding him through a syringe. His jaw surgery at the height of my pregnancy was tiring, painful, and demanding for both of us. We had tried every type of broth, protein drink, or pureed food to satisfy his hunger. At one point, we even had meat and potatoes in a blender. Don't judge.

After I pulled up to the ice cream shop yet again, trying to convince the person behind the counter that the ice cream shake was not for me, I realized I didn't care what they thought. My focus was on my husband. I understood his desire and wanted his hunger to be satisfied.

Hunger is the natural means our body has for craving something. If we lack food or water, our body responds with longing for what can fill the void. We begin to eat or drink, and the pangs begin to disappear, and slowly we feel full, attaining satisfaction.

Although our physical need for food is powerful and absolutely essential, our heart and soul has another need. Through the pages of this book, we have been talking about an inner longing that each human has: the craving inside our heart is for value, love, and purpose. Inside every man is the desire to be known and to matter. You have read the pages of this book because something inside of you connects with this idea of craving more. We not only long to understand our own identity and purpose, but we realize along the way that longing is tied to knowing who God is. We are created to crave Him.

Every morning, I wake up and immediately desire a good cup of coffee, and if I am honest, a really good pastry. You might consider me a closet foodie who loves great food and the beauty that defines it. If we look further, I will tell you I prefer to eat it on a simple white plate so all the colors and textures can be appreciated. After all, we eat with our eyes too! Maybe you are the same way? You have a favorite pastry, snack, or item that causes your mouth to water when you think of it. Mouth watering, your thoughts are on that thing, that smell, or the place where it's served just right. I get it. I have already lost you in your imagination. You want to put down this book and go get it! Right?

Everyone has something they crave. Besides ice cream shakes, my husband craves a specific dessert his Nana used to make, and every birthday he gets his "cheese pie." My son sends me thank you texts (with pictures) at midnight when he gets home and sees his favorite pasta dish in the fridge. One of my daughters loves fresh cranberry scones, while the other gets that gleam in her eye when I mention that I made "cheesy" potatoes. We all have room in our being for the thing we love, but it goes beyond just really liking it. There is a powerful longing that goes beyond appreciation; it becomes something we passionately desire.

HUNGER AND THIRST

Research done by the National Library of Medicine describes the differences and similarities the human body experiences due to hunger and thirst. Their studies[14] explain that the cravings or sensations we experience are similar for both needs. When we start to crave food or something specific, it can be our way of interpreting thirst, not just craving for food. The feelings are the same and our body needs both.

David, the worshiper, and king mentioned in the Bible, understood this concept of craving. He consistently wrote songs and poems that described how much his soul longed to know God and experience His love. David even compared the desire to the way a deer pants after water. This craving or thirst comes from our soul, which the Hebrew language describes as the seat of our appetite.[15] From our soul, inside our being is the desire, emotion, or longing that comes like an appetite.

In a song penned by David, he describes it this way: "O God of my life, I'm lovesick for you in this weary wilderness. I thirst with the deepest longings to love you more, with cravings in my heart that can't be described. Such yearning grips my soul for you, my God! I'm energized every time I enter your heavenly sanctuary to seek more of your power and drink in more of your glory" (Psalm 63:1-2 TPT).

David realized that the purpose of his life, his deepest longing, was to love God. It was why he was created: to love and be loved by

God. This man knew the simple life of tending sheep, experienced defeating a giant – which was miraculous in every way – and later became King of all Israel, holding power and wealth. He knew all seasons and aspects of what this world had to offer, and yet from youth to death He craved to love God and know God's goodness (drink more of His glory). In the wilderness and in the sanctuary, David was consumed by hunger and thirst for God's presence. It is the bread and water he wanted to live on.

WHAT DO WE CRAVE

Do you know the saying *you are what you eat*? The Bible talks about the idea of having an appetite for good things. The Message version of Matthew 5:6 showcases this well when it says, "You're blessed when you've worked up a good appetite for God. He's food and drink, the best meal you'll ever eat." I love that!

It is incredible to think that happiness (the deeper meaning of the word blessed) comes when you develop an appetite for God. Another version puts it this way: "Blessed [joyful, nourished by God's goodness] are those who hunger and thirst for righteousness [those who actively seek right standing with God], for they will be [completely] satisfied" (AMP). It is not just small hunger pangs we are talking about. The Greek word *peinao*[16] actually paints a picture of earnest desire or famished craving. There is joy when we realize that He is what we are desperate for. He is our nourishment.

Inside our soul, we have a place that craves everything about God: His truth, His love, His acceptance, and the words He speaks. They are life to our weary souls. In fact, Jesus is called the Bread of Life. He has many roles or names, some of which are Savior, King, Prince of Peace, Good Shepherd, and Friend. When we experience Him as all those things, our lives are transformed.

For this Italian girl, bread is life. If all I had access to was bread and water, I could survive. If there was oil or butter to go with the bread...bliss! I love that God knows this about me, and so He created me to love one thing even more than bread. He gave me a desire, in the deepest part of my core, for one thing: His voice. We were created not just to crave physical food, but spiritual food. We were created to live on more than just bread but on every word that comes from the mouth of God.

Jesus is referred to as the Word. Those who knew Him best understood that His words were life giving. They vowed their devotion to Him, not wanting to go anywhere else because no one else "has the words of eternal life" (John 6:68 NIV). God gave us Jesus, the Bread of Life, to stir up hunger, and the Holy Spirit as living water to quench our thirst. These two pictures remind us where we get our source and refreshment from. He alone is our daily portion, the One we can draw from and partake of each day for truth, life, value, purpose, identity, and guidance.

Communion with Him is the only way we can successfully live each day in abundance. Just like we need breakfast daily, our connection to Him is dependent on daily refilling. God satisfies, but in the contentment, a desire for more is created. Spiritual hunger is just as important as natural hunger. As we get up every morning, our souls and our spirit require fresh food.

Our lives are more than just a body. Our souls will only be able to thrive if they are nourished by God's voice (see Matthew 4:4). Each fresh daily Word He speaks is what our appetite should crave! His active voice allows us to move past the pressing needs and distractions of this life; the responsibilities and urgencies can become our focus. His voice is what helps us navigate through all of that and pursue greater things.

Just as the Israelites had fresh mana every morning, we have the living voice of God speaking to us through the Holy Spirit. Those fresh utterances (called *Rhema* in Greek)[17] give us clear directions into possibilities. We can move past any limitation if we fill up on the words of God. This means anything written in His Word or actively spoken from His Spirit! They are fuel for our next steps so we can move toward the promises we pursue. His words are worth snacking on throughout the day like a protein bar, and they are worth sitting at the table to feast with family.

Remember, we were made for eternity. At our core is the desire to do impossible things. Why? Because we are designed like God who eats impossible for breakfast! Though this world seems ordinary, we were made for extraordinary pursuits. We were designed for a destiny full of promises and possibilities. With every bite of God's promises and truth, our hunger increases. We realize quickly that spiritual hunger is constant; just when you think you are satisfied, our desire for more becomes insatiable.

Inside our soul, we have a place that craves everything about God: His truth, His love, His acceptance, and the words He speaks.

Questions and Reflections
...to ponder on your way to possibilities!

➤Can you relate to the desire to be known or to matter? Is it a constant ache or a subtle pang that only comes to the surface at key moments?

➤Can you pinpoint moments you have felt as the Psalmist David felt, when he said, "O God of my life, I'm lovesick for you in this weary wilderness. I thirst with the deepest longings to love you more, with cravings in my heart that can't be described. Such yearning grips my soul for you, my God! I'm energized every time I enter your heavenly sanctuary to seek more of your power and drink in more of your glory" (Psalm 63:1-2 TPT).

➤What does it look like in your life to "live by every word that comes from the mouth of God"?

➤Do you agree with this statement? "God satisfies, but in the contentment, a desire for more is created." How have you experienced this in your own life?

➤Have you heard God speak "fresh words" to your heart before? Do you have a hunger for more of that?

18

POSTURED FOR MORE

KISSING MY BABIES GOODBYE, exhausted from life but expectant, I boarded a plane for Africa. If you had told me a year before that I would be leaving behind three very small children to travel around the globe, I would have laughed. Traveling was not something new. I had traveled internationally a few times already, but the surprise would have been about the timing of this trip. With three kids under four, you wouldn't expect a stay-at-home mom of toddlers to be en route to the other side of the world.

Why was I flying so far away? Because a few months before I stood at the back of a church service, felt something inside me shift, and then heard God whisper, "You want to go." Those were not the words I was expecting my brain to process. Africa? Most often it's the place that comes out of people's mouths when they say, "God, I will serve You, but...please don't send me there." Here I was, headed off to that place, and I was so excited.

From a young age, I always lived in the middle between sensible and a good adventure. There are definite moments when risk would not be in my vocabulary. I prefer safety and security, and yet there is also a craving deep inside for possibilities. When a prompting from

God's voice was mixed in, there was an urgency in my soul to go for it. It wasn't just an obligatory need to obey, it was more an excitement that He has invited me to go somewhere or achieve something. I have found it's not always easy to take the first step, but the reward is worth it. The craving in my heart, to live wholeheartedly in pursuit of all God has for me, is what is left when you peel back all the nervousness and uncertainty. Deep down, there is a hunger for more.

When we encounter God's Spirit of truth we are drawn to know more. We aren't satisfied with just one mystery solved. We are hungry to know more of this truth that defies worldly philosophy. Those who are hungry have the desire to move deeper into this incredible and tangible thing we now know as God's presence. We don't want to stand on the outside of the invisible veil. No, we have been told there is no longer a veil; nothing inhibits our entrance into His incredible joy, love, peace, and wonder. So, we press into the inner chamber. We walk in because we are hungry. We are more than hungry; we are ravenous for more of Him. This taste of wonder, love, and incredible joy is just the start. After that first bite, we realize we have been left with a desire for more wonder, more presence, more God.

There is a posture necessary as we go after more. It's a position of expectancy, anticipating what lies on the other side of possibility. My journey to Africa reminds me of a story I love in the Bible. Just after the Israelites made their way out of bondage in Egypt, they wandered for 40 years in the desert. From that place of circling, complaining, and waiting, a handful of men got the opportunity to go explore the land they had been waiting to occupy.

POSTURED FOR COURAGE

Joshua and Caleb were two of the men who were chosen to go into the land and then report back to the others what they found. I could spend an entire chapter or book on this story, but instead I will point out that Caleb was a man described as wholly following God (see

Joshua 14:9). Looking at his life, we see that he postured himself to be faithful, courageous, and trust God's Word. He saw God do miracles, and he carried the hope and optimism of what could be. Caleb was not pulled down into pity, fear, or disobedience. Instead, he postured his life to live in the opposite spirit than the others (see Numbers 14:24). Because of the way he lived his life, he set himself up for a grand inheritance.

As we read this incredible story, we see that all of the Israelites who saw God miraculously deliver them from slavery died in the wilderness except Joshua and Caleb. They wandered and saw the wonder of a mighty God but chose to stay in limitation. Moses didn't even cross over into the Promised Land. Instead, he passed the baton to two men who lived from faith and wholehearted obedience to God's Word. Joshua and Caleb were the only ones who, after 40 years in the wilderness, accessed their inheritance!

Just like Abraham having to wait for his promised heir, Caleb watched decades pass before his feet stood on the ground he was promised. He had carried hope and promise in his heart regarding the land he spied out years earlier. His life was filled with grumbling, disobedient people around him, but Caleb was patient, chose his attitude, and lived in daily encounters with God so he could receive the land that had been assigned to him!

Life in the desert wasn't easy. Life in our neighborhoods are just as messy. We have grumbling, rebellion, disappointments, and lack if we choose to only see those things. However, like Caleb, we can choose to be a man (or woman) who postures our lives in the opposite way.

Here is what I believe we can learn from Caleb: live life unafraid! Caleb was one who saw possibility even in the impossible. Like the rest of the spies, he spent 40 days checking out the land; a land full of milk and honey and filled with abundantly large fruit. Yes, the people living there were tall and powerful, but Caleb silenced all of the people who were reporting in fear. Instead, Caleb spoke in courageous faith and said, "We can certainly do it" (Numbers 13:30 NIV).

Courage looks like confidence!

Caleb postured himself with courage and wholehearted obedience. While others doubted their ability to conquer the land because of visible circumstances, Caleb and Joshua trusted God and went in with a heavenly perspective. If they can do it, so can you! There will be naysayers who tell you that your time is over. Maybe you have people in your life who say, "We'll never make it. It'll never work." They might try to discourage you because your problems are too big. Culture around you will say it can't be done, but guess what? You have the choice to agree with those who doubt you can obtain your promises, or you can come in the opposite spirit!

There is a moment, right now as you are reading this, where you must decide if you can cross from fear to faith. There is a line in the wilderness that separates you from the Promised Land. We can be like the culture around us with limited sight, or we can live unafraid and pursue the *more* God has promised us. There is abundance and fruitfulness that has been promised and is ready to be occupied.

What are the things you're contending for? Are you okay with being stuck in pity, insecurity, doubt, or fear? You can live a life with limits, or you can make a shift towards the opposite and stir up courage like Caleb did. There has to be a moment where we push past fear or intimidation and choose confidence that God is who He says He is and has created us to go after greater things! That is the very definition of courage: being confident in the face of fear. Courage is the largeness of heart (not our physical organ, but our inner world).

Courage looks like not comparing our life to others!

You may feel the need to do something that is contrary to what those around you are doing. If we compare our lives to others, we get bogged down by doubt, fear, worry, and frustration. Comparison kills courage. We are not to measure our choices by what others say. Our direction comes from God's voice. What has He promised? What has He spoken? We live our lives in obedience to Him, not setting our eyes on those around us. Like the other spies said, the people of the land were big and powerful and they felt like grasshoppers. Comparison shrinks our view of who God has made us. We must not allow others to determine that.

Courage looks like not giving up!

Caleb followed wholeheartedly, which in Hebrew means "to fill, accomplish or complete."[18] Caleb didn't give up. He didn't allow the circumstances to dictate his reaction. He lived from a place internally that knew he was not defeated or discouraged. He chose not to lose heart, but instead knew that we must not "become weary in doing good, for at the proper time we will reap a harvest if we do not give up" (Galatians 6:9). If we keep doing what is right, the Lord will fill us with His love and strengthen us with endurance!

Caleb was courageous! He encouraged the people to move away from fear and into courage because the Lord was with them. He lived with a determined heart to face the enemy head on. Though others were discouraged and fearful, Caleb and Joshua knew this was their land to occupy. Because of that courage, they were the only two from that generation to attain their promise. Their courage and trust allowed them to receive an inheritance.

COURAGE IS NOT SAFE!

I wish I could say courage was easy. There may be moments when choosing courage doesn't have a deadly outcome. There are less dramatic courage moments, but I don't think having courage can ever be categorized as easy. It always takes pushing past insecurities and fears. Largeness of heart demands that our inner world knows who God is and whose we are. It requires a steadfast determination that says no matter what, I will obey God's voice and fight for what's right.

Like Joshua and Caleb, I understand what it looks like to be in new territory, treading carefully as you walk. In Africa, I was thousands of miles from my family but present in the moment. It had been a full day out in the village, and I had experienced every type of emotion. There had definitely been a heaviness as we walked through this village. I could tangibly feel the influence of the demonic principalities who were not pleased as we walked into their territory to take ground. Incredible moments happened along the way as well, but we had to push past a tangible darkness that tried to keep us from sharing freedom with those who needed to hear it that day.

Walking alone in a village where you sense the invisible opposition is not easy. We ventured out to tell anyone who would listen how Jesus had changed our lives. Yet every step felt like slamming our face into an unseen wall. Throughout the day, God kept whispering to me, "Have courage. Take this land." *How, God? How are we supposed to do that?* Then, came the moment I knew. I turned to my translator and told him what I had been feeling, and he agreed we needed to stop, pray, and worship. Moments later, we came upon a hut. I don't even remember how we knew or why we were there. I imagine the translator knew this was the one house in the area that could help.

We stepped inside their small dark hut, accompanied by a cow, chickens, and meager possessions, and we worshiped. They had already been in their hut praying. We stepped into their faith-filled space and joined our voices with theirs to contend for their land. The presence of God was so thick in that room, I didn't want to leave.

At the end of the day, as I walked toward the main road to wait for the van that had dropped us off earlier that day, a mob of angry men came at us with walking sticks raised. They were yelling and waving their sticks at us with determination. They had found out we were there, and were angry we had stepped onto their land with a message about Jesus. We now saw with our eyes what our hearts had been sensing all day: darkness.

At that moment, I felt like I had no courage in me. Panic flooded my mind, pushing out all the thoughts of the miracles I had just witnessed and the lives I had just seen touched by the presence of God. The only thought left in my head was, *I am going to die in this dusty brown field and never see my children again.* I began walking faster and praying under my breath. I cried out to Jesus to save us, and tried to stay behind the one friend who was also returning from the village.

I wish I could say I became unafraid but I can't. I definitely was strengthened by God's Spirit and felt moments of peace come, but the shift in my inner world never fully moved from fear to faith. At that moment I thought I had no courage. When a van pulled up saying they were full and we would have to wait for the next one, tears started spilling from my eyes. They were going to leave me there.

Maybe you are thinking, I have not, nor will I ever be in that kind of situation. That may be true, but you have seen angry looks, heard vindictive accusations hurled at you, and been unfriended or yelled at. Maybe your social media page was spammed with angry posts because you made one comment standing up for life and darkness wanted to silence you. Maybe you felt opposition from that family member who likes to criticize everyone, including you, for every decision that differs from how they would do it. Or maybe you, too, have felt like you have been left alone, not protected, not loved, and not saved from that horrible situation.

Like the eight other spies who accompanied Joshua and Caleb, the enemy wants us to feel like grasshoppers surrounded by those who have power over us. His goal is to keep us from inheriting the spaces in our life, the relationships around us, businesses, ministries, and freedom. He wants us to stay limited in our thinking so we will give up on moving forward.

Courage has a cost. It requires us to give up believing the voices that come at us and only cling and hold onto the one voice that matters. His name is Jesus. I was not the best example of courage that day. Yes, I was there and obedient to God. Technically I pushed past my fears and fought the opposition by praying and worshiping. But in the face of real danger, my courage was tested. The giants seemed to grow, and I felt a little like a grasshopper.

I am writing this, so obviously you know I survived. I was able to leave the area that had been taken over by angry men. I was driven to safety and eventually went home to my family. Though I never lost courage because I pushed past the fear, the couple in their hut praying and worshiping for their land were the real courageous ones. They remained. They didn't escape the opposition. They took a risk every day to love God in an area filled with people who greatly oppose Him. They were taking ground and expanding their territory one prayer at a time.

Our choices, our attitudes, and our ability to endure the hard moments in life are not just victories for us; they are plots of land we occupy and then leave to future generations as their inheritance. Your children and grandchildren will benefit from the choices you make now to leave behind limitations and believe for the impossible. Posturing our lives for abundance looks like the declaration Joshua made before crossing over to go after the land. He encouraged the people to, "Consecrate yourselves, for tomorrow the Lord will do amazing things among you" (Joshua 3:5 NIV).

We get to choose today to set ourselves in position to be a better friend to God and like Caleb, receive inheritance into all of those things. Let's set our hearts on what God will do, not just the things He hasn't done. A posture of courage looks ahead with hope and excitement for possibilities. Caleb was invited into legacy, and because he postured his heart to follow God wholly, that land became one of promises and promotion for a legacy of men and women who followed. Even a prostitute was invited into promise.

Our ability to endure the hard moments in life are not just victories for us: they are plots of land we occupy and then leave to future generations as their inheritance.

Questions and Reflections
...to ponder on your way to possibilities!

❧

➤Are you sensing a stirring inside your soul for more? Are there things in your internal world that have shifted? Maybe lies or limitations that no longer have you stuck? If so, ask God to breathe onto those places. If not, ask God to keep shaking and threshing, revealing any lies that are holding you captive.

➤Have you begun to position yourself for possibilities? What does that look like for you?

➤In what areas have you seen yourself step foot into the promises of God? What areas of your life have been granted access to promise?

➤What are the things you're contending for? What areas are you still fighting for and believing to see God fulfill in your life?

➤How can you apply the following verse to your situations? "Do not become weary in doing good, for at the proper time we will reap a harvest if we do not give up" (Galatians 6:9). Have you ever had to push past tangible darkness?

19

PASSIONATE PURSUIT

"I AM a hunter of beauty and I move slowly, and I keep the eyes wide, every fiber of every muscle sensing all wonder and this is the thrill of the hunt and I could be an expert on the life full, the beauty meat that lurks in every moment. I hunger to taste life. God."[19] I love that quote; it describes an insatiable passionate pursuit.

It's not long before the journey of hunger turns to hunting. Our meandering stroll turns into hot pursuit of this wonder we tasted. Red lights are our past; green is bright and bold and gives us permission to go and not stop. Pursuit involves intent and drive. We are hungry for more of God, and so we pursue with passion, letting go of what distracts or limits us. No prize is attained when we take our eyes off our pursuit.

HUNGER PURSUES

There was a woman I needed to find. Walking the streets with my eyes alert, I went about my day trying to find her. You see, there is a posture we need if we want to see God do more in our lives. It is one of seeking from a place of expectation. Months before ever setting foot overseas, I had postured myself for more. I wanted to hear God speak to me about my life, but also speak about what I would be stepping into. In those moments of humble seeking, God showed up!

In my prayer time, God showed me a woman's face. I saw her smile and eyes, but most of all I was drawn to this pattern in the dress she was wearing. As I prayed about it more, I began hearing specific promises that God had for this woman I'd never met. I didn't even know if she really existed, but I wrote down all of God's words, because I believe that when God speaks, even if we don't understand it right away, there is value in His voice. His words are life to the hearer, and I knew there was a portion of the message for me, but also for something greater!

As God spoke about her, there was a deep love, and I felt the invitation He was extending to draw her to Himself. There was hope, love, and purpose in this message. I carried this burning message in my heart as I went village to village, with pursuit and intent to find this woman who couldn't be a figment of my imagination. I had told my friends with me on the trip about the woman, and they prayed with me that I would find her. I was also nervous because finding her would require me to be bold enough to step across cultural lines and unfamiliarity to give her the message God had shown me. But wasn't that why I was there?

I understood a little about how Caleb and Joshua felt. I, too, was in a foreign land, stepping out in faith because I loved God with my whole heart and told Him I would follow Him anywhere. It took courage for me to leave behind my family, and it would take courage to carry promises into those villages.

She wasn't in the airport or the villages. I looked for her around the streets where we shopped and traveled. Then, one day she walked into the room. There she was standing in front of me, wearing the same dress I had seen in my vision. My jaw dropped and I froze. The woman was the manager of the hotel we were staying in. I couldn't believe it. The timing wasn't right to approach her right then, but I walked back to my room praying for God to give me courage and the opportunity to talk to her.

That night, we were invited to come to a special ceremony. It was a cultural tradition which included popcorn and coffee. God had me at popcorn (and coffee), but what excited me more was that this woman was hosting us. I told my friends, they prayed with me, and then we set off to meet her. My only goal was to seek her out and share the message God had sent me to give.

She was there to greet us. My friends sat farther away so I could take the seat right next to her. She explained the ceremony. Her staff came in and served us, and she and I began talking. Our conversation was very natural, and we learned about each other. I began to weave God's message into our dialogue, and then I felt the Holy Spirit stir me to step out in courage.

I told her about the vision I had. As I spoke about her dress and my prayers, tears sprang into her eyes. I shared God's heart for her and told her the truth that He believed about her. More tears. We talked and she shared some of her story. She also shared how loved and seen she felt by God knowing that He had sent an American woman halfway around the world just to give her a message.

What I have not shared are the days of attack we encountered before I was able to deliver this message. We arrived at the hotel, and suddenly there was no water. Vultures flocked near our window almost mocking us and signaling to us they were circling and searching for prey. Not to mention the early morning wake-up calls from the nearby mosque. With so many signs of opposition, my roommate and I worshiped, prayed, and released life into this land held by darkness, drought, and death. Shifting the atmosphere, we began to claim this land for God's Kingdom.

We seek God alone. In doing so, we cling to His promises for us. They are for our everyday life and home, but they are also for the lands and people He wants us to touch. Every place where we set our feet becomes places for His love and abundance to reach. Our job is to remain strong and courageous. We cling to hope and cling to God's promises because He has places and spaces to give us as an inheritance. It may be physical land, businesses, people groups, innovations, children, or something else. No matter what, there are inheritances we have yet to attain but are called to occupy.

Caleb and Joshua spent 40 days spying out the land, but another 40 years before they occupied it. Let that sink it! Their inheritance had to be fought for and in some ways waited for. But with obedience, they kept seeking God's lead and followed with their whole hearts. Then they were given their promise.

HUNGER DRAWS OUT

Our hunger draws out His abundance. It reminds me of the act of siphoning gas. Though I haven't tried it with gas, I have had to unclog a hose using a similar principle. With the way gas prices have been rising, people are desperate, and I have seen posts on neighborhood forums of this happening right down the street. Of course I don't want anyone to use these principles and go out and break the law. Instead, apply this simple process to your pursuit of abundance.

This concept begins with two vessels. The idea is to draw the liquid from one vessel to the other. This is done by putting one side of a hose into a higher vessel and the other side in a lower vessel. The hose is just the conduit. Pressure, gravity, or in our analogy, hunger, builds and draws out or transfers the substance. I am not a scientist, nor do I plan to prove the details of the process, but what I can say is that if you create internal pressure, usually by sucking the air out of the hose, flow will start and continue if you are drawing from a higher place.

Our hunger gets the internal pressure building in our spiritual life. We begin to breathe in desire for greater things, higher things, and then we see abundance begin to flow into our lives. The key is drawing from a higher elevation. Remember, altitude matters.

Just before my 40th birthday, I was in a place of great spiritual hunger. My desire to spend time with God and read His Word was at a high. In my hunger, I felt my inner world drawing and pulling from heaven. It made me want more. Apart from working and taking care of my family, I spent all of my extra time desiring more of God.

What does that look like? I was reading my Bible and setting aside time to listen more intently. I was reading books by others about pursuing God's heart more intentionally. I had decided to do a 40-day fast to cleanse myself of some of the *extra and unnecessary* things and had decided it would involve food and media. I gave up my TV binge watching, which at the time was really my only source of relaxation time. In addition to movies, I gave up certain types of food. There are lots of great resources about fasting, though this chapter is not about that. What I do want to say is fasting postures our heart in humility and for hunger. We give up things so our focus and attention can be placed elsewhere. My desire was for more of God. As Bill Johnson puts it, "Heaven Invading Earth."[20] I want more of heaven as I walk this earth.

Just before this decision to do a 40-day fast, I had a deep longing to go on another mission trip. Just like the story which started this chapter, my heart stirred with possibility to see God do above and beyond what I had seen Him do. I told my husband and we prayed about it. He told me if I wanted to go, he would support me. So, I told all my family and friends that all I wanted for my 40th birthday was to go to India, and I started raising money.

My attention was focused on hearing His voice for my next season and pursuing His heart. My desire for Him and this trip grew. You see, when we give up natural things and redirect our focus, our hunger grows for the unseen. It's not just giving up food, and I didn't go on a diet. I postured my heart for hunger. When we "look away from the natural realm and we focus our attention *and expectation* onto Jesus who birthed faith within us...[he] leads us forward into faith's perfection" (Hebrews 12:2 TPT).

Those 40 days were transformational. I saw a different layer of my own humanity, and ultimately I saw a more beautiful picture of God's heart. I heard His voice more clearly. I had visions, dreams, and encounters with the Holy Spirit that filled me up! I was like the lower vessel that was empty and waiting, drawing, and pulling on the abundance of heaven that sat at the higher elevation.

Hunger motivates a passionate pursuit of God which changes the internal atmosphere of our heart. That transformation then overflows into the external atmosphere of our lives. If you want to see change around you, you must first change from inside. That happens as we allow the goodness of God to lead us and perfect us! Heaven's resources transform us and make us whole. Our completeness is like a prize. Our pursuit of God's heart and voice changes us from the inside out and fills us up to overflowing so we can pour out refreshing in our families, churches, neighborhoods, cities, and nations!

HUNGER INHERITS

Pursuing possibilities comes when we are sure of what God has said. This confidence allows us to step out in courage and see God do incredible things. I knew God had promised to show me incredible things in India. I pursued His heart, asking what kind of things He wanted to do in me and through me. Then, from that posture of humility, I left to conquer lands – sharing God's Kingdom with the most remote places on the planet. It required courage and complete dependance on God's voice. Ultimately, there was intense hunger to be part of the *more* I knew God was capable of.

There is one woman who became part of Joshua and Caleb's story. She lived in the land the Israelites were going to conquer, which meant she was about to have her entire life turned upside down. Yet this prostitute named Rahab, who was limited by her occupation and status, also had a hunger inside her for more. Rahab's house had frequent visitors, and because of this, the men sent in to spy on the land probably thought they could stay there without alerting the king. However, the king found out strangers had gone to Rahab's house, so she was told by the king to turn in the spies. At that moment, she had a choice to follow the king of the land or pursue the desire in her heart to know the King above all others. Rahab sent word to the king that the men who had stayed with her had left, and that they could be pursued outside the city gates.

But Rahab had actually hidden the men on her roof under stalks of flax. In her own words, she had hidden them because she knew God was giving them this land. She saw how fearful her people were because of the other nations that had been destroyed. Hunger stirred inside her to be part of God's people, so she struck a deal.

The spies promised to save her and her family if she helped them escape. She let down a rope through the window so they could climb down out of the city. This is such an incredible picture of hunger. She was siphoning courage, promise, and inheritance because she knew they had power and authority to save her family and secure her inheritance.

The scarlet cord she hung from her window was a picture of hope. The Hebrew word for rope or cord used in this story (in Joshua 2) also means "a portion or region of land." Rahab was securing her land, her family, and ultimately her future by extending a rope when the Israelites came back to occupy the land. You can read the entire story later, but for now, stop and realize Rahab and her family were saved because of her *hunger*.

Fast forward, Caleb inherited the land of Hebron, which was the land he first went in to explore. For those of you who love history, this piece of land was south of Jerusalem's walls, set in the hills. The Hebrew name of the city means "friend." To me this is such a picture of God's faithfulness. God knew Caleb was His devoted friend, and so God gave him this special land that was rich in heritage. This friend of God inherited the palace where Abraham and his entire family are buried. It was the area of land deemed as *the Promised Land.*

Many years after Caleb resided in that region, David would come on the scene. He was a descendant of the same Rahab who had been saved during Joshua and Caleb's journey. The woman who had pulled down heaven's resources because of hunger allowed generations after her to dwell safely in that land. There in that place, David was anointed king of Judah and then later, king of Israel. David and generations after him would be listed in the family tree of Jesus! Caleb's inheritance of courage and faith built a residence on Abraham's credit account of righteousness, allowing many after them to see promise and promotion.

We have the opportunity to leave a legacy for future generations. Our hunger makes hope secure. Hebrews tells us we, too, can, "Show the same diligence [all the way through] so as to realize *and* enjoy the full assurance of hope until the end" (Hebrews 6:11 AMP). We are designed to crave constant pursuit. Our hope is that God knows us personally and has set us on this earth to carry a message of hope. This hope allows us to "imitate those who through faith and patience inherit what has been promised" (Hebrews 6:12 AMP). We become part of the story that began back with Abraham. We become part of the chain effect and list of men and women who passionately pursued possibility.

One hungry person can't change *the* world, but one hungry person can change *their* world. We can impact our circles. We can reflect God's goodness and nature to those around us. Each one of us, in our own unique way, reflects our Creator. By design, we each have pieces of who God is. One of our best pursuits could be defined as discovering the multifaceted dimensions of who God is. I think we can all agree that God is complex; we could spend our entire life learning more about who he is. This life *can* be about that! In fact, it should be one of our deepest desires in this life. We also get to discover who we are and who we are called to become so we can add value to our world.

By understanding who God is, what His voice sounds like, and what His guidance looks like, we can tap into doing life well.

Becoming aware of our hunger, our dreams, and His purposes for our lives, we will see the limitless opportunities still ahead. Your good days haven't expired. No matter your season, He still has good plans for you. There are promised lands to be occupied!

The red lights of your past do not define your destiny, and though the journey is hard, we can choose hope! We can embrace every situation and see the fullness of God in every moment and every attitude. Why? Because in His presence is the fullness of joy, and He is EVERYWHERE. His goodness and love never to leave you; in fact, He promises they will follow you all the days of your life (Psalm 23:6). Don't laugh, but I imagine them running after me wherever I go...more like chasing after me!

God is ready to invite us into the hallway and show us more of who He is. Intimacy has always been His goal. His desire is to know us and for us to know Him...really well. He wants to journey with us. He lays out straight paths for us; paths that are metaphoric for our relationship with Him. We are not on a rocky path or a dirt road. We are not on a concrete sidewalk in suburbia. We are on a journey – a journey in the middle of Him.

And so, we end where we began. Our life journey is to inherit the promises of God. It is not just one end goal, nor is it just one promise. There are many promises, which come with many provisions, making every one of our steps matter. Each act of kindness, love, and service reveals the things that God desires to fulfill in our lives. Every bill paid, chore completed, or task finished was an opportunity to discover another aspect of who God is for you in the mundane. He is with us in the moments in between, thrilled we have stepped off the curb of complacency to run toward Him and all the possibilities yet to be realized. He wants us to live without limits.

We have been designed for a destiny of more in our DNA. You have permission to step off the curb like Abraham, go higher like David, and inherit and occupy that space like Caleb. You have permission to move away from the familiar and into the deeper and greater things God desires you to experience. There is hope and confidence our destiny is comprised of successive nows! Each step, living in the moment as we pursue His heart and voice, will lead us to more of who we are because we pursue more of who He is. He is our *more*.

We are designed for a destiny of more.

Questions and Reflections
...to ponder on your way to possibilities!

➤What does the following statement mean? "Hunger draws out His abundance." Is there an example of this in your life?

➤What are some ways you can draw from higher elevation? What promises can you attach your faith to bringing heaven down to your situations?

➤What does the following verse mean to you and your situations? "Look away from the natural realm and we focus our attention *and expectation* onto Jesus who birthed faith within us...[he] leads us forward into faith's perfection" (Hebrews 12:2 TPT).

➤Like Rahab, what promises or cords of hope can you secure in your life to position yourself for safety and life?

➤Think about this statement: "One hungry person can't change *the* world, but one hungry person can change *their* world." What things are you committing to changing in your world? What is one practical step towards that?

He is...

Patiently leading us on a journey toward destiny. Though obstacles come our way, His goodness turns them into moments of adjustment, realigning our core beliefs about who HE is and who WE are. He provides opportunities as we partner with Him, and we're growing in our ability to choose actions as great as our...

Attitude, which has been seasoned with grace, joy, and power for the journey. Perspective changes our view of our environment and shifts the atmosphere. If we let thankfulness and joy be honed within, it flings open the doors so we can gain entrance into...

Throne Room encounters that birth passion and greater intimacy with our King. Our King, seated on His throne, delights in knowing us and delights in revealing Himself to us when we knock, seek, and fall on our face in worship. Such love stirs up greater...

Hunger deep in our souls. We become insatiable and realize we are not at the beginning or end of our destiny. Instead, we are on a continual journey that involves a passionate pursuit of Him.

You have been designed for a destiny of more. He is our **PATH.** In Him, we find all we need for our pursuit of *more. Are you ready?*

ACKNOWLEDGEMENTS

So many incredible people have been part of my life and journey. Their stories have impacted and inspired my own. I want to highlight a few who were specifically involved in seeing this project through to completion!

I have already dedicated and thanked my incredible husband, children, and parents for their involvement, but I will say again, without your love, support, and provocation you wouldn't be reading this now. You hold my heart and have helped me become who I am today! There are not enough words. I love you.

Bruce Sr.: Thank you for being one of my biggest cheerleaders. Your encouragement to pursue what God made me for will stay with me...always. You are one of my favorite story tellers, and I hope I made you proud!

Ashley and Rachelle: I love you both so much! I am so grateful God gave me beautiful and talented sisters. I appreciate that you did not squash my crazy dreams but teased me through them and cheered me on!

Havilah, Francis, and The Author School coaches/peeps: After one click, who knew I would find such an amazing group of world changers? I want to extend a huge thank you to all of you (especially my mastermind group) for inspiring me, cheering me on, and walking with me through the pain and delight of birthing this special project. The H.A.S. community was priceless. You authors are true gems with a story to tell!

Connie and Canvas Intercession Team: You ladies are in my corner! Thank you for praying with me and for me through the highs and lows of this process. I appreciate your commitment to speak life and cover my family with your faith-filled prayers.

Susan and Mary: You started as prayer partners, and then gladly added editors-in-crime to your resume. I cannot thank you enough for the hours of reading, proofing, and suggesting so I could relate my message with excellence.

Krista: I prayed you in, and thank God I found an editor who was willing to dive into the deep end with me. I appreciate your professionalism, your discernment, and attention to detail. Thank you for helping me state my message with impact and clarity.

Joe: Who else would I call but the best? Thank you for partnering with me to make my author and website photos fun and meaningful. I appreciate you taking time away from the family and your crazy wedding shoots to help me...not to mention work miracles (wink).

Kristina and Oralia: Our coffee dates, hikes, and body marking adventures are priceless. Thank you for encouraging me, crying with me, and laughing with me—— a lot. I am grateful for our friendship, and that we get to rejoice together and believe for God's goodness to abound.

Michelle: You consistently asked questions, provoked thought, and cheered me on. Thank you for being excited with me for what God is doing in my life and staying hungry (with me) for more!

Heather: Your lifelong friendship is invaluable. You have walked with me through many challenges and fought battles alongside me through many disappointments. I know we have a cloud of witnesses cheering us both on.

Miguel and Debbie: I thank God for the way you carry God's Spirit of Revival, and the way you constantly encourage. You are faithful to affirm and honor both my gifts and voice. Muchas gracias.

Osil and Rachel: God brought you into my life at just the right moment of my process. Your example, encouragement, and inspiration were the tangible voice of the Father that I needed to finish birthing my message.

Mark and Shell: You both were there at the inception of my book dreams (so many years ago). You both spoke into that assignment and provided space for its genesis. Thank you for walking alongside me in my journey and even paving the way for some of my steps!

John and Hope: You pastored us through some of our most prominent highs and lows. We are grateful for your constant encouragement to have faith and see God's goodness in the land of the living. You witnessed God redeem so much of our story, and we stand with you to see Him redeem yours!

Ben and Katie: Basketball and a global pandemic started it all! Thank you for your friendship, leadership, and involvement in my book journey. My sabbatical from worship ministry turned into a book writing adventure, which is now birthing even more. Thank you for your prayers, love, and support.

I could thank so many, but I stop and give praise, honor, and glory to the ONE who gave it all for me, and so I will lay it all down for Him. No words could adequately thank my good Father who loves me, wrote eternity in my heart, speaks willingly, and walks adventurously with me toward the more He has for me. To say I am eternally grateful is true, but truer still is the fact that He is making me eternally minded. I pray that I never walk a day on this earth silent. Rather, *"I'll trust in you to help me. Nothing will stop me from praising you to magnify your glory! I couldn't begin to count the times you've been there for me. With the skill of a poet, I'll never run out of things to say about how you faithfully kept me from danger. I will come forth in your mighty strength, O my Lord God. I'll tell everyone that you alone are the perfect one. From my childhood, you've been my teacher, and I'm still telling everyone of your miracle-wonders! God, now that I'm old and gray, don't walk away. Give me the grace to demonstrate to the next generation all your mighty miracles and your excitement, to show them your magnificent power"* (Psalm 71:14-18 TPT).

Endnotes

1. "Wonder Definition & Meaning." *Merriam-Webster*, Merriam-Webster, https://www.merriam-webster.com/dictionary/wonder.

2. "Shunt Definition & Meaning." *Merriam-Webster*, Merriam-Webster, https://www.merriam-webster.com/dictionary/shunt.

3. "Immanuel - Bible Meaning and Definition 'God with Us.'" *Biblestudytools.com*, https://www.biblestudytools.com/dictionary/immanuel/.

4. "Repose Definition & Meaning." *Merriam-Webster*, Merriam-Webster, https://www.merriam-webster.com/dictionary/repose.

5. *Strong's Greek: 2722. Κατέχω (Katechó) -- to Hold Fast, Hold Back*, https://biblehub.com/greek/2722.htm.

6. *Strong's Greek: 1680. Ἐλπίς (ELPIS) -- Expectation, Hope*, https://biblehub.com/greek/1680.htm.

7. *Strong's Greek: 5287. Ὑπόστασις (Hupostasis)*, https://biblehub.com/greek/5287.htm.

8. "Abide Definition and Meaning - Bible Dictionary." *Biblestudytools.com*, https://www.biblestudytools.com/dictionary/abide/.

9. "Strong's Greek: 3306. Μένω (Menó)." *Strong's Greek: 3306. Μένω (Menó) -- to Stay, Abide, Remain*, https://biblehub.com/greek/3306.htm.

10. "Charles R. Swindoll Quotes (Author of the Grace Awakening)." *Goodreads*, Goodreads, https://www.goodreads.com/author/quotes/5139.Charles_R_Swindoll.

11. "Exploring Series with Shawn Bolz." *Your Footprint on This Earth Will Change the World with Lauren Hasson (S:2 - Ep 30)*, https://exploringtheprophetic.libsyn.com/your-footprint-on-this-earth-will-change-the-world-with-lauren-hasson-s2-ep-30.

12. "Encounter Definition & Meaning." *Merriam-Webster*, Merriam-Webster, https://www.merriam-webster.com/dictionary/encounter.

13. Oscar Wilde

14. McKiernan, Fiona, et al. "Relationships between Human Thirst, Hunger, Drinking, and Feeding." *Physiology & Behavior*, U.S. National Library of Medicine, 6 Aug. 2008, https://www.ncbi.nlm.nih.gov/pmc/articles/PMC2467458/.

15. "H5315 - Nep̄eš - Strong's Hebrew Lexicon (KJV)." *Blue Letter Bible*, https://www.blueletterbible.org/lexicon/h5315/kjv/wlc/0-1/.

16. "Strong's Greek 3983." *Strong's Greek: 3983. Πεινάω (Peinaó) -- to Hunger, Be Hungry*, https://biblehub.com/greek/3983.htm.

17. "Strong's Greek: 4487." *Strong's Greek: 4487. Ῥῆμα (Rhéma) -- a Word, by IMPL. A Matter*, https://biblehub.com/greek/4487.htm.

18. "Strong's Hebrew 4390." *Strong's Hebrew: 4390. מָלֵא (Male or Mala) -- to Be Full, to Fill*, https://biblehub.com/hebrew/4390.htm.

19. Voskamp, Ann. *One Thousand Gifts: A Dare to Live Fully Right Where You Are*, W Publishing Group, an Imprint of Thomas Nelson, Nashville, TN, 2021, pp. 71–72.

20. Bill Johnson

ABOUT THE AUTHOR

Kiersten Clegg is a prophetic voice, worship leader, teacher, and author who values hearing God's voice. She has raised three children (including homeschooling) and taught the next generation of musicians. She has sown into women, worship ministries, prayer teams, and prophetic culture to help others step into freedom and purpose. Her passion is to use her prophetic gift to encourage, equip, and inspire others to hear God's voice. Kiersten, her husband, and their three children reside in beautiful San Diego, where they enjoy serving their community and the local church.

WWW.KIERSTENCLEGG.COM

facebook.com/kierstencleggauthor

instagram.com/kiersten.clegg

www.ingramcontent.com/pod-product-compliance
Lightning Source LLC
Chambersburg PA
CBHW070657130626
46553CB00005B/1737